GENTLE

....

MARIE WALLIN

CONTENTS

GENTLE

FOREWORD

GENTLE is the second collection using my BRITISH BREEDS yarn and introduces the four new colours for the season - 'Silver Birch', 'Pale Oak', 'Blossom' and 'Foxglove'. You can read in more detail about my yarn and the new colours in a feature at the back of the book.

The GENTLE collection is a combination of traditionally inspired Fair Isle and Moorish ornamental design. The garment shapes are contemporary in styling, making them an essential addition to your Winter wardrobe. Teamed with your favourite tweeds, corduroys or denims, they will look amazing!

We photographed GENTLE at the pretty Walnuts Farm in rural East Sussex. The farmhouse in particular evoked the sense of calm that I was looking for, giving the collection a beautiful, tranquil and peaceful feel. I'm sure you will agree that Peter captured the spirit of this collection with his wonderful photography and Georgia, well she just gets more beautiful the older she becomes!

I am very proud of this collection with some of the designs becoming my personal favorites! I also think that the addition of the four new colours has helped make the designs more intense and alive.

I really do hope that you enjoy GENTLE as much as I enjoyed designing it!

Happy knitting!

PRIMROSE

...Is surprisingly the first all over Fair Isle design, knitted in the round, that I have designed since I left Rowan over five years ago! The shape of this design is fitted so if you wish to have a looser feel then I suggest that you knit the next size up.

GENTLE

VERONICA
COWL

....

This is a great design to practise your Fair Isle skills if you lack the confidence to knit a garment. It is knitted in the round and the motifs are placed in a small repeating pattern.

CAMPION

··

This is another favourite design of mine. The shape is slightly oversized and the elongated fronts create a very flattering look. It can be worn open or fastened with a brooch or pin.

GENTLE

POPPY SCARF

This lovely design is entirely knitted in the round creating a fabric which is double thickness, making a very warm and cosy scarf. The design could easily be shortened and joined at both ends to create a cowl.

GENTLE

FOXGLOVE

...is a very pretty design, with a lace and twisted stitch body and a simply patterned yoke. The longer length is very flattering to wear but it could be easily shortened to a standard length sweater if desired.

HONEYSUCKLE

· ·

This beautiful traditional Fair Isle cardigan is also included in my MEADOW collection. When I first designed the cardigan, I liked it so much that I decided to re-colour it using my BRITISH BREEDS yarn. I hope you agree that the result is rather lovely!

GENTLE

GENTLE

MISTLETOE
TAM

....

A pretty Fair Isle tam, easy to knit and to wear. Knitted in the round, this is a design suitable for knitters that are new to stranded colour work.

GENTLE

GENTLE

IVY

....

...is the first of two single colour textured designs. It is
a lovely cable and twisted stitch design which has an
oversized shape and three-quarter length sleeves. I think
it looks great in the new SILVER BIRCH colour!

BRAMBLE

This is a lovely design inspired by Moorish tiles seen in the grand mansions of southern Spain. It has been designed to be shorter in length but can be lengthened easily by just adding a pattern section.

GENTLE

LUPIN SOCKS

....

I decided to add a sock design to this collection after the popularity of my NORAH FAIRE ISLE SOCKS, which I did for two day workshops and a kit. These are rather pretty socks, largely due to the addition of SILVER BIRCH, BLOSSOM and FOXGLOVE, three of the new colours.

ORLA

....

...is my re-colour of the design I did for the 10th Anniversary Shetland Wool Week Annual. That version is crocheted using Jamieson's of Shetland SPINDRIFT and when I designed it, I liked it so much that I decided to rework it using my BRITISH BREEDS yarn. The result is a slightly stronger, more autumnal colourway than the pretty and more muted Shetland design.

GENTLE

BEECH

....

...is another favourite of mine as it's so lovely to wear!
The very narrow back neck shaping makes the fronts
of the cardigan drape in a flattering way. The cardigan
is interesting to knit as the main body is worked by
picking up stitches from the side edge of the cabled
bottom section. It looks equally great worn fastened
with a brooch or pin or worn loose.

GALLERY

PRIMROSE

Main Image Pages
Front cover, 8, 10, 11
Pattern Page 64

VERONICA
COWL

Main Image Pages 12, 13,
14,15
Pattern Page 68

CAMPION

Main Image Pages 16, 18, 19
Pattern Page 70

POPPY SCARF

Main Image Pages 20, 21,
22, 23
Pattern Page 74

FOXGLOVE

Main Image Pages 24, 25,
26, 27
Pattern Page 76

HONEYSUCKLE

Main Image Pages 28, 29, 30,
31, back cover
Pattern Page 79

MISTLETOE
TAM

Main Image Pages 6, 32,
34, 35
Pattern Page 84

IVY

Main Image Pages 36, 38, 39
Pattern Page 86

BRAMBLE

Main Image Pages 40, 42,
43, 44, 62
Pattern Page 90

LUPIN SOCKS

Main Image Pages 46, 48, 49
Pattern Page 94

ORLA

Main Image Pages 50, 51, 52,
53, 54, 114
Pattern Page 97

BEECH

Main Image Pages 5, 57, 58,
59, 60
Pattern Page 102

42 [43: 44: 44: 44] cm
(16½ [17: 17¼: 17¼: 17¼] in)

53 [54.5: 56: 57.5: 58.5] cm
(21¾ [21½: 22: 22¾: 23] in)

42.5 [50: 55: 63: 68] cm
(16¾ [19½: 21½: 25: 26¾] in)

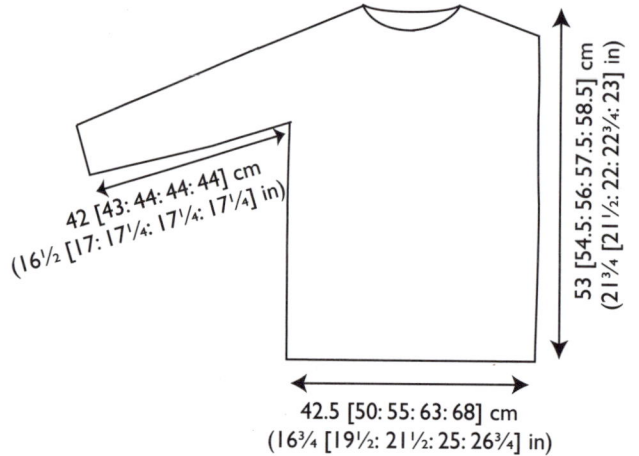

	S	M	L	XL	XXL	
To fit bust	81-86	91-97	102-107	112-117	122-127	cm
	32-34	36-38	40-42	44-46	48-50	in

Marie Wallin British Breeds

		S	M	L	XL	XXL	
A	Quince	3	3	3	4	4	x 25gm
B	Dark Apple	2	2	2	3	3	x 25gm
C	Eau de Nil	1	2	2	2	2	x 25gm
D	Wood	2	2	2	3	3	x 25gm
E	Foxglove	1	2	2	2	2	x 25gm
F	Raw	1	1	2	2	2	x 25gm
G	Rose	1	2	2	2	2	x 25gm
H	Blossom	2	2	3	3	3	x 25gm
I	Mallard	1	2	2	2	2	x 25gm
J	Lime Flower	2	2	2	2	2	x 25gm
K	Russet	1	2	2	2	2	x 25gm
L	Silver Birch	2	2	2	2	2	x 25gm
M	Chestnut	1	1	2	2	2	x 25gm
N	Pale Oak	1	1	1	2	2	x 25gm

Needles

2¾mm (no 12) (US 2) circular needle
3¼mm (no 10) (US 3) circular needle
Set of 4 double-pointed 2¾mm (no 12) (US 2) needles
Set of 4 double-pointed 3¼mm (no 10) (US 3) needles

Tension

28 sts and 29 rounds to 10 cm measured over patterned st st

using 3¼mm (US 3) circular needle.

Special note – Georgia is wearing size S in the photographs and it is more fitted than the usual size S – see size diagram.

BODY (worked in one piece to armholes)
Using 2¾mm (US 2) circular needle and yarn A cast on
240 [288: 312: 360: 384] sts.
Taking care not to twist cast-on edge and placing a marker on first st of next round to denote beg and end of rounds, cont as folls:
Round 1 (RS): *K1, P1, rep from * to end.
This round forms rib.
Keeping rib correct and joining in and breaking off colours as required, cont in rib in stripes as folls:
Round 2: Using yarn A.
Rounds 3 and 4: Using yarn B.
Rounds 5 and 6: Using yarn I.
Rounds 7 and 8: Using yarn D.
Rounds 9 and 10: Using yarn E.
Rounds 11 and 12: Using yarn G.
Rounds 13 and 14: Using yarn H.
Rounds 15 and 16: Using yarn J.
Rounds 17 and 18: Using yarn K.
Rounds 19 and 20: Using yarn L.
Rounds 21 and 22: Using yarn M.
Rounds 23 and 24: Using yarn N.
Rounds 25 and 26: Using yarn C.
Rounds 27 and 28: Using yarn B.

Rounds 29 and 30: Using yarn H.
Rounds 31 and 32: Using yarn D.

Rib should measure 6cm from cast on edge.
Change to 3¼mm (US 3) circular needle.
Beg and ending rounds as indicated, using the **fairisle technique** as described on the information page and repeating the 24 st patt repeat 10 [12: 13: 15: 16] times around each round, cont in patt from chart for body, which is worked entirely in st st (K every round), as folls:
Work 62 rounds.
Round 63: Patt 56 [68: 74: 86: 92] sts and slip these sts onto a holder (for left back), patt 9 sts and slip these 9 sts onto a safety pin (for left underarm), patt 111 [135: 147: 171: 183] sts and slip these sts onto another holder (for front), patt 9 sts and slip these 9 sts onto another safety pin (for right underarm), patt rem 55 [67: 73: 85: 91] sts and slip these sts onto another holder (for right back).
Break yarns and remove marker.

SLEEVES
Using set of 4 double-pointed 2¾mm (US 2) needles and yarn A cast on 54 [56: 58: 58: 62] sts.
Distribute sts evenly over 3 of the 4 needles and, taking care not to twist cast-on edge and placing a marker on first st of next round (to denote sleeve "seam"), cont as folls:
Work rounds 1 to 32 as given for body.
Change to double-pointed 3¼mm (US 3) needles.
Beg and ending rounds as indicated, using the **fairisle technique** as described on the information page, repeating the 24 st patt repeat twice around each round and repeating the 91 row patt repeat throughout, cont in patt from chart for sleeve **beg with chart row 7 [3: 1: 1: 1]**, which is worked entirely in st st (K every round), as folls:
Work 3 rounds.
Next round: Inc in first st, patt to last st, inc in last st.
Working all increases as set by last round, inc 1 st at each end of 5th and every foll 5th round to 78 [72: 82: 94: 98] sts, then on every foll 6th round until there are 90 [96: 96: 98: 102] sts, taking inc sts into patt.
Work 3 rounds, ending after chart round 13.
Next round: Patt 5 sts and slip these 5 sts onto a safety pin (for underarm), patt 81 [83: 87: 89: 93] sts and slip these sts onto another holder (for sleeve), patt rem 4 sts and slip these sts onto same safety pin as first 5 sts – 9 sts now on underarm safety pin.
Break yarns.

YOKE
With RS facing, using 3¼mm (US 3) circular needle and yarn A, K across sts on holders as folls: K across 56 [68: 74: 86: 92] sts on left back holder dec 0 [1: 2: 3: 0] sts evenly, K across 81 [83: 87: 89: 93] sts on left sleeve holder dec 0 [0: 2: 3: 0] sts evenly, K across 111 [135: 147: 171: 183] sts on front holder dec 0 [2: 4: 5: 0] sts evenly, K across 81 [83: 87: 89: 93] sts on right sleeve holder dec 0 [0: 2: 3: 0] sts evenly, then K across 55 [67: 73: 85: 91] sts on right back holder dec 0 [1: 2: 2: 0] sts evenly.
384 [432: 456: 504: 552] sts.

Place marker on first st – this is centre back st.
Using yarn A, K 0 [1: 1: 1: 1] round.
Beg and ending rounds as indicated, using the **fairisle technique** as described on the information page and repeating the 24 st patt repeat 16 [18: 19: 21: 23] times around each round, cont in patt from chart A, which is worked entirely in st st (K every round), as folls:
Work rounds 1 to 19.
Using yarn A, K 1 [2: 2: 2: 2] rounds.
Now work chart rounds 20 to 26.
Next round: Using yarn L, K0 [0: 18: 21: 24], (K1, K2tog, K2 [2: 1: 1: 1], sl 1, K1, psso, K1) 48 [54: 60: 66: 72] times, K0 [0: 18: 21: 24]. 288 [324: 336: 372: 408] sts.
Using yarn L, K 0 [1: 1: 1: 1] round.
Beg and ending rounds as indicated, using the **fairisle technique** as described on the information page and repeating the 12 st patt repeat 24 [27: 28: 31: 34] times around each round, cont in patt from chart B, which is worked entirely in st st (K every round), as folls:
Work rounds 1 to 12.
Using yarn L, K 0 [1: 1: 1: 1] round.
Work rounds 13 to 17.
Using yarn I, K 0 [0: 0: 1: 1] round.
Work rounds 18 to 23.
Using yarn I, K 0 [0: 0: 1: 1] round.
Next round: Using yarn J, K0 [0: 25: 21: 24], (K1, K2tog, K1 [1: 0: 0: 0], sl 1, K1, psso) 48 [54: 57: 66: 72] times, K0 [0: 26: 21: 24]. 192 [216: 222: 240: 264] sts.
(**Note**: As the number of sts decreases, change to double-pointed needles.)
Using yarn J, K 0 [0: 1: 1: 1] round.
Beg and ending rounds as indicated, using the **fairisle technique** as described on the information page and repeating the 6 st patt repeat 32 [36: 37: 40: 44] times around each round, cont in patt from chart C, which is worked entirely in st st (K every round), as folls:
Work rounds 1 to 10.
Using yarn J, K 0 [0: 0: 1: 1] round.
Work rounds 11 and 12.
Using yarn C, K 0 [0: 0: 1: 1] round.
Work rounds 13 to 19.
Next round: Using yarn L, K16 [4: 5: 0: 0], (K2tog, sl 1, K1, psso) 40 [52: 53: 60: 66] times, K16 [4: 5: 0: 0]. 112 [112: 116: 120: 132] sts.
Using yarn L, K 4 [4: 6: 5: 8] rounds.
Work neckband
Change to double-pointed 2¾mm (US 2) needles.
Now work in rounds of rib as given for body in stripes as folls:
Rounds 1 and 2: Using yarn A.
Rounds 3 and 4: Using yarn B.
Rounds 5 and 6: Using yarn I.
Rounds 7 and 8: Using yarn A.
Using yarn A, cast off in rib.

MAKING UP
Press as described on the information page.
See information page for finishing instructions, joining both body and sleeve underarm seams by grafting tog each set of 9 sts left on safety pins.

KEY

- □ A. Quince
- × B. Dark Apple
- – C. Eau de Nil
- ■ D. Wood
- ▲ E. Foxglove
- • F. Raw
- ◢ G. Rose
- ○ H. Blossom
- ▼ I. Mallard
- ∕ J. Lime Flower
- ◣ K. Russet
- ∪ L. Silver Birch
- ● M. Chestnut
- △ N. Pale Oak

CHART C

6 st patt rep

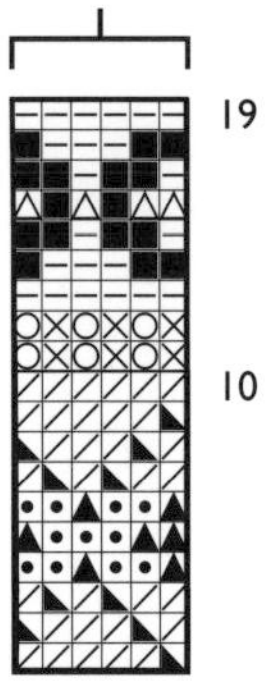

CHART A

24 st patt rep

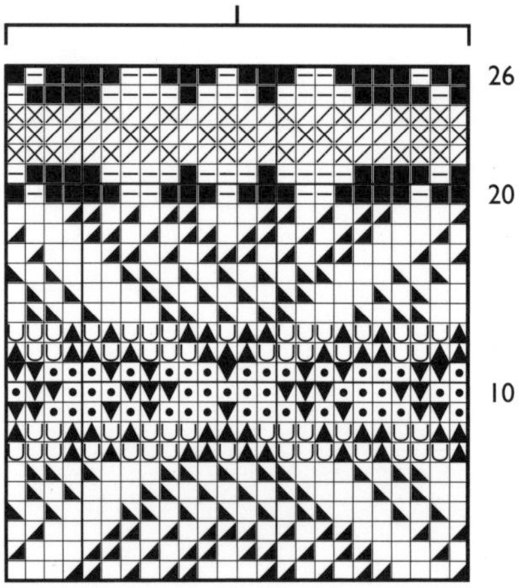

CHART B

12 st patt rep

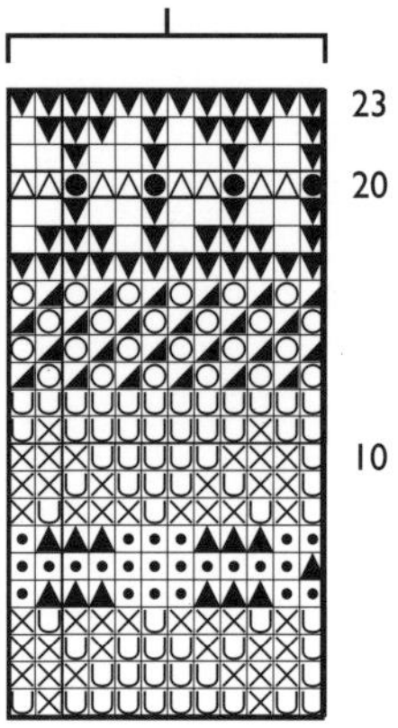

BODY CHART

24 st patt rep

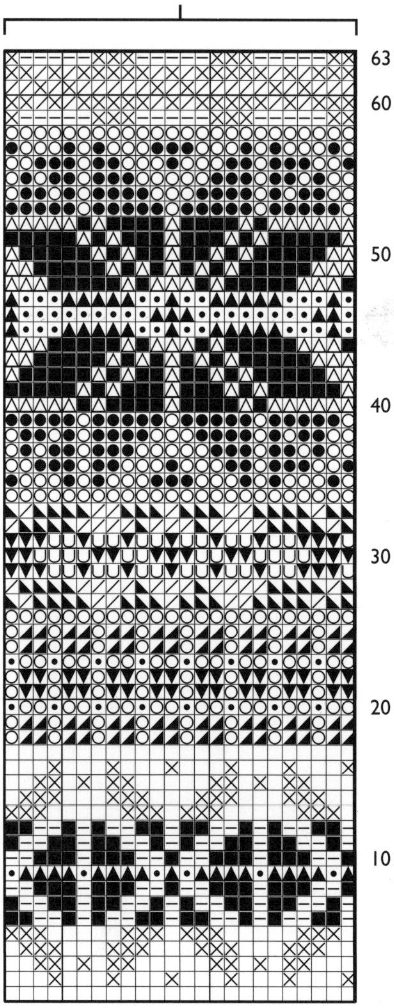

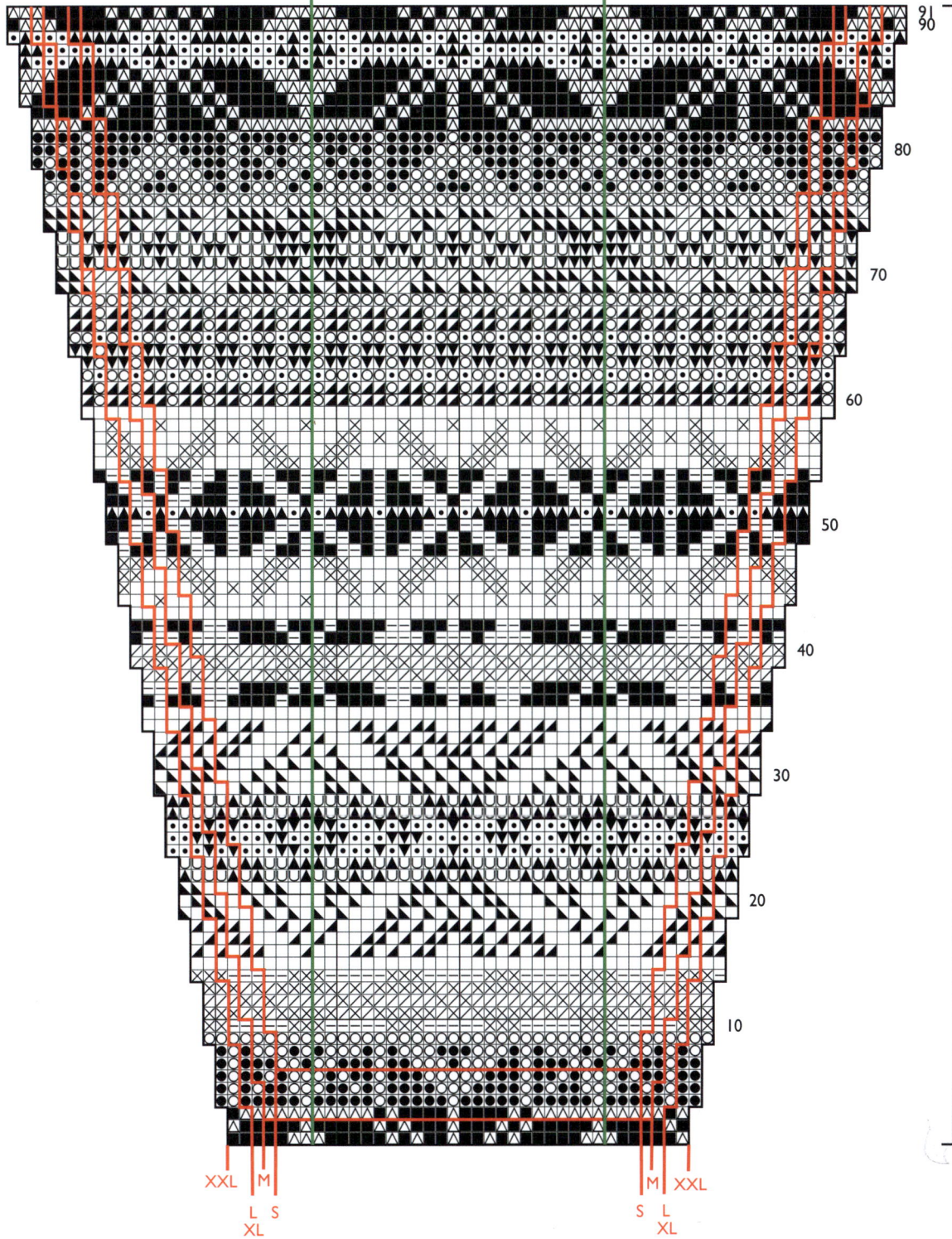

SLEEVE CHART

24 st patt rep

91
90

80

70

60

50

40

30

20

10

91 round patt rep

XXL   M
   L   S
   XL

         M   XXL
      S L
         XL

VERONICA COWL ● ●

Size

One size only

Marie Wallin British Breeds

A	Wood	1	x 25gm
B	Eau de Nil	1	x 25gm
C	Pale Oak	1	x 25gm
D	Mulberry	1	x 25gm
E	Rose	1	x 25gm
F	Blossom	1	x 25gm
G	Woad	1	x 25gm
H	Foxglove	1	x 25gm
I	Raw	1	x 25gm
J	Lime Flower	1	x 25gm
K	Chestnut	1	x 25gm
L	Quince	1	x 25gm
M	Russet	1	x 25gm
N	Dark Apple	1	x 25gm
O	Silver Birch	1	x 25gm

Needles

2¾mm (no 12) (US 2) circular needle – 60 cm (24 in) fixed length
3¼mm (no 10) (US 3) circular needle – 60 cm (24 in) fixed length

Tension

28 sts and 29 rounds to 10 cm measured over patterned st st using 3¼mm (US 3) circular needle.

Finished size

Completed cowl measures 78.5 cm (31 in) in circumference all round and 26 cm (10¼ in) deep.

COWL
Bottom welt

Using 2¾mm (US 2) circular needle and yarn G cast on 220 sts.
Taking care not to twist cast-on edge, work in rounds as folls:
Round 1 (RS): *K1, P1; rep from * to end.
This round forms rib.
Place marker on first st of round just knitted to denote beg and end of rounds.
Cont in rib for a further 6 rounds.
Next round: Purl.
Next round: Knit.
Break off yarn G.
Change to 3¼mm (US 3) circular needle.
Joining in and breaking off colours as required, using the **fairisle technique** as described on the information page and repeating the 20 st patt repeat 11 times around each round, work rounds 1 to 63 of chart, which is worked entirely in st st (K every round).

Break off yarns.

Top welt

Change to 2¾mm (US 2) circular needle and join in yarn G.

Next round: Knit.

Next round: Purl.

Work 7 rounds in rib as given for bottom welt.

Cast off in rib.

FINISHING

Press as described on the information page.

Sew in any loose ends on WS of cowl.

KEY

- ■ A. Wood
- • B. Eau de Nil
- × C. Pale Oak
- ● D. Mulberry
- ▲ E. Rose
- ○ F. Blossom
- ◢ G. Woad
- + H. Foxglove
- □ I. Raw
- ╱ J. Lime Flower
- ▼ K. Chestnut
- Ι L. Quince
- ∪ M. Russet
- ◣ N. Dark Apple
- − O. Silver Birch

20 st patt rep

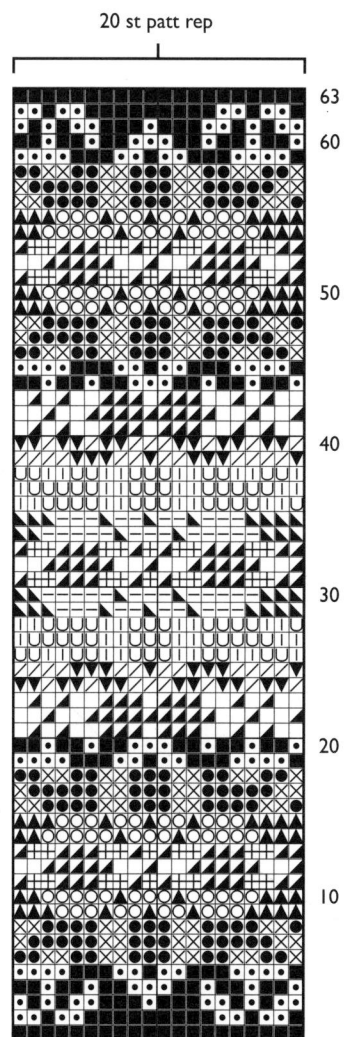

54 [56: 58: 60: 62] cm
(21¼ [22: 22¾: 23½: 24½] in)

44 [45: 46: 47: 48] cm
(17¼ [17¾: 18: 18½: 19] in)

48 [53: 59: 65: 72] cm
(19 [20¾: 23¼: 25½: 28¼] in)

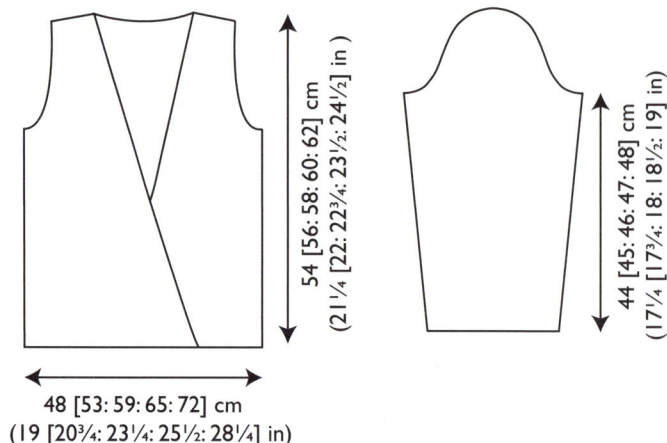

	S	M	L	XL	XXL	
To fit bust	81-86	91-97	102-107	112-117	122-127	cm
	32-34	36-38	40-42	44-46	48-50	in

Marie Wallin British Breeds

		S	M	L	XL	XXL	
A	Rose	3	3	3	4	4	x 25gm
B	Foxglove	2	2	2	2	2	x 25gm
C	Wood	2	2	2	3	3	x 25gm
D	Pale Oak	1	1	2	2	2	x 25gm
E	Chestnut	2	2	2	2	2	x 25gm
F	Blossom	2	2	2	2	3	x 25gm
G	Russet	2	3	3	3	3	x 25gm
H	Quince	2	2	2	2	2	x 25gm
I	Dark Apple	2	3	3	3	3	x 25gm
J	Lime Flower	2	2	2	2	2	x 25gm
K	Mallard	2	2	2	2	2	x 25gm
L	Silver Birch	1	1	1	1	2	x 25gm
M	Eau de Nil	1	1	1	1	1	x 25gm
N	Raw	1	1	1	1	1	x 25gm
O	Mulberry	1	1	1	1	1	x 25gm

Needles

1 pair 2¾mm (no 12) (US 2) needles
1 pair 3¼mm (no 10) (US 3) needles
2¾mm (no 12) (US 2) circular needle

Tension

28 sts and 29 rows to 10 cm measured over patterned st st using

3¼mm (US 3) needles.

BACK
Using 2¾mm (US 2) needles and yarn A cast on
135 [149: 165: 183: 201] sts.
Row 1 (RS): P1, *K1, P1, rep from * to end.
Row 2: K1, *P1, K1, rep from * to end.
These 2 rows form rib.
Work in rib for a further 4 rows, ending with RS facing for next row.
Change to 3¼mm (US 3) needles.
Beg and ending rows as indicated, using the **fairisle technique** as described on the information page and repeating the 68 row patt repeat throughout, cont in patt from chart, which is worked entirely in st st beg with a K row, as folls:
Work 94 [96: 100: 104: 106] rows, ending after chart row 26 [28: 32: 36: 38] and with RS facing for next row. (Back should meas approx 34 [35: 36: 37: 38] cm.)
Shape armholes
Keeping patt correct, cast off 6 [7: 8: 9: 10] sts at beg of next 2 rows. 123 [135: 149: 165: 181] sts.
Dec 1 st at each end of next 7 [9: 11: 13: 15] rows, then on foll 3 [4: 5: 7: 8] alt rows, then on foll 4th row.
101 [107: 115: 123: 133] sts.
Work 33 [33: 31: 27: 27] rows, ending after chart row 10 [16: 22: 28: 34] and with RS facing for next row. (Armhole should meas approx 18 [19: 20: 21: 22] cm.)

Shape shoulders and back neck
Next row (RS): Cast off 6 [7: 7: 8: 9] sts, patt until there are
23 [25: 28: 31: 34] sts on right needle and turn, leaving rem sts on
a holder.
Work each side of neck separately.
Keeping patt correct, dec 1 st at neck edge of next 4 rows **and at
same time** cast off 6 [7: 8: 9: 10] sts at beg of 2nd and foll alt row.
Work 1 row.
Cast off rem 7 [7: 8: 9: 10] sts.
With RS facing, slip centre 43 [43: 45: 45: 47] sts onto a holder
(for front band), rejoin yarns and patt to end.
Complete to match first side, reversing shapings.

LEFT FRONT
Using 2¾mm (US 2) needles and yarn A cast on
93 [107: 123: 141: 159] sts.
Work in rib as given for back for 6 rows, ending with RS facing for
next row.
Change to 3¼mm (US 3) needles.
Beg and ending rows as indicated, cont in patt from chart as folls:
Work 2 rows, ending with RS facing for next row.
Shape front slope
Keeping patt correct, dec 1 st at end of next row, then at same
edge on foll 10 [16: 22: 28: 34] rows, then on foll 21 [23: 29: 35: 34]
alt rows, then on 9 [7: 4: 0: 0] foll 4th rows. 52 [60: 67: 77: 90] sts.
Work 3 [3: 1: 3: 1] rows, ending after chart row 26 [28: 32: 36: 38]
and with RS facing for next row.
Shape armhole
Keeping patt correct, cast off 6 [7: 8: 9: 10] sts at beg and dec
1 [1: 0: 1: 1] st at end of next row. 45 [52: 59: 67: 79] sts.
Work 1 row.
Dec 1 st at armhole edge of next 7 [9: 11: 13: 15] rows, then on
foll 3 [4: 5: 7: 8] alt rows, then on foll 4th row **and at same time**
dec 1 st at front slope edge on 3rd [3rd: next: 3rd: next] and foll
0 [0: 0: 0: 7] alt rows, then on 3 [4: 6: 7: 5] foll 4th rows.
30 [33: 35: 38: 42] sts.
Dec 1 st at front slope edge **only** on 2nd [2nd: 4th: 6th: 6th] and
1 [1: 0: 0: 0] foll 4th row, then on 2 [2: 2: 1: 1] foll 6th rows, then
on foll 8th row. 25 [28: 31: 35: 39] sts.
Work 7 rows, ending after chart row 10 [16: 22: 28: 34] and with
RS facing for next row.
Shape shoulder
Cast off 6 [7: 7: 8: 9] sts at beg of next row, then 6 [7: 8: 9: 10] sts
at beg of foll 2 alt rows.
Work 1 row.
Cast off rem 7 [7: 8: 9: 10] sts.

RIGHT FRONT
Using 2¾mm (US 2) needles and yarn A cast on
93 [107: 123: 141: 159] sts.
Work in rib as given for back for 6 rows, ending with RS facing for
next row.
Change to 3¼mm (US 3) needles.
Beg and ending rows as indicated, cont in patt from chart as folls:
Work 2 rows, ending with RS facing for next row.
Shape front slope
Keeping patt correct, dec 1 st at beg of next row, then at same
edge on foll 10 [16: 22: 28: 34] rows, then on foll 21 [23: 29: 35: 34]

alt rows, then on 9 [7: 4: 0: 0] foll 4th rows. 52 [60: 67: 77: 90] sts.
Complete to match left front, reversing shapings.

SLEEVES
Using 2¾mm (US 2) needles and yarn A cast on
67 [71: 73: 73: 75] sts.
Work in rib as given for back for 6 rows, ending with RS facing for
next row.
Change to 3¼mm (US 3) needles.
Beg and ending rows as indicated and starting with chart row **39**,
cont in patt from chart as folls:
Inc 1 st at each end of 7th [7th: 7th: 5th: 5th] and every foll 8th
[8th: 8th: 6th: 6th] row to 91 [93: 101: 83: 91] sts, then on every
foll 10th [10th: 10th: 8th: 8th] row until there are
95 [99: 103: 107: 111] sts, taking inc sts into patt.
Work 9 rows, ending after chart row 26 [28: 32: 36: 38] and with
RS facing for next row. (Sleeve should meas approx
44 [45: 46: 47: 48] cm.)
Shape top
Keeping patt correct, cast off 6 [7: 8: 9: 10] sts at beg of next
2 rows. 83 [85: 87: 89: 91] sts.
Dec 1 st at each end of next 7 rows, then on every foll alt row
until 55 sts rem, then on foll 7 rows, ending with RS facing for
next row. 41 sts.
Cast off 4 sts at beg of next 4 rows.
Cast off rem 25 sts.

MAKING UP
Press as described on the information page.
Join both shoulder seams using back stitch, or mattress stitch if
preferred.
Front band
With RS facing, using 2¾mm (US 2) circular needle and yarn A,
beg and ending at front cast-on edges, pick up and knit
167 [175: 183: 192: 201] sts evenly up entire right front opening
edge, and 5 sts down right side of back neck, K across
43 [43: 45: 45: 47] sts on back holder inc [inc: dec: inc: inc] 1 st at
centre, then pick up and knit 5 sts up left side of back neck, and
167 [175: 183: 192: 201] sts evenly down entire left front opening
edge. 388 [404: 420: 440: 460] sts.
Row 1 (WS): K1, P2, *K2, P2, rep from * to last st, K1.
Joining in and breaking off colours as required, cont as folls:
Row 2: Using yarn C K3, *P2, K2, rep from * to last st, K1.
Last 2 rows form rib.
Cont in rib in stripes as folls:
Row 3: Using yarn C.
Rows 4 and 5: Using yarn E.
Rows 6 and 7: Using yarn G.
Rows 8 and 9: Using yarn I.
Rows 10 and 11: Using yarn K.
Rows 12 and 13: Using yarn O.
Rows 14 and 15: Using yarn A.
Rep rows 2 to 15 once more, then row 2 again, ending with **WS**
facing for next row.
Using yarn C, cast off in rib (on **WS**).
See information page for finishing instructions, setting in sleeves
using the set-in method.

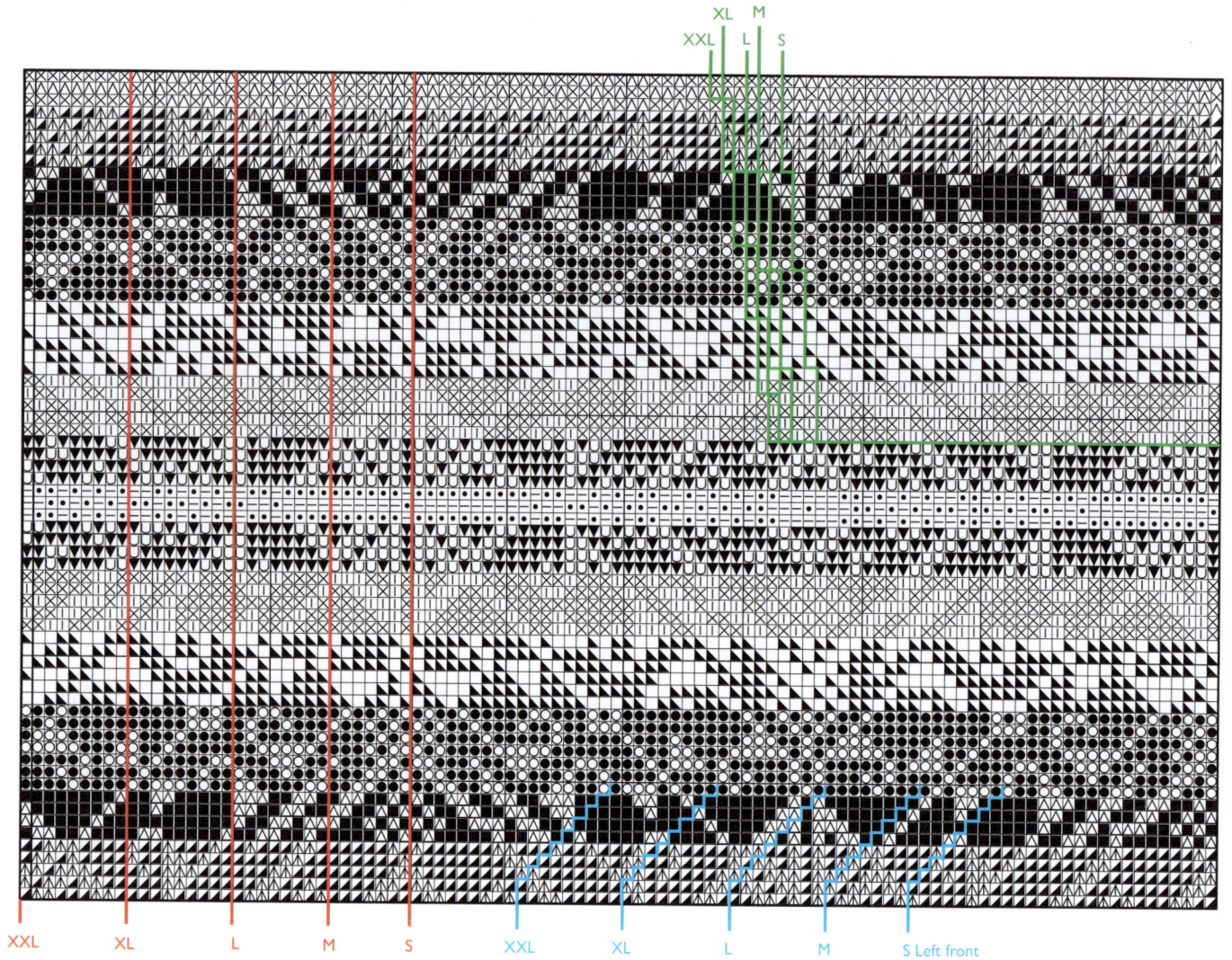

KEY

◢	A. Rose	✕	I. Dark Apple
∧	B. Foxglove	∣	J. Lime Flower
■	C. Wood	▼	K. Mallard
△	D. Pale Oak	∪	L. Silver Birch
●	E. Chestnut	—	M. Eau de Nil
○	F. Blossom	•	N. Raw
◣	G. Russet	∧	O. Mulberry
▢	H. Quince		

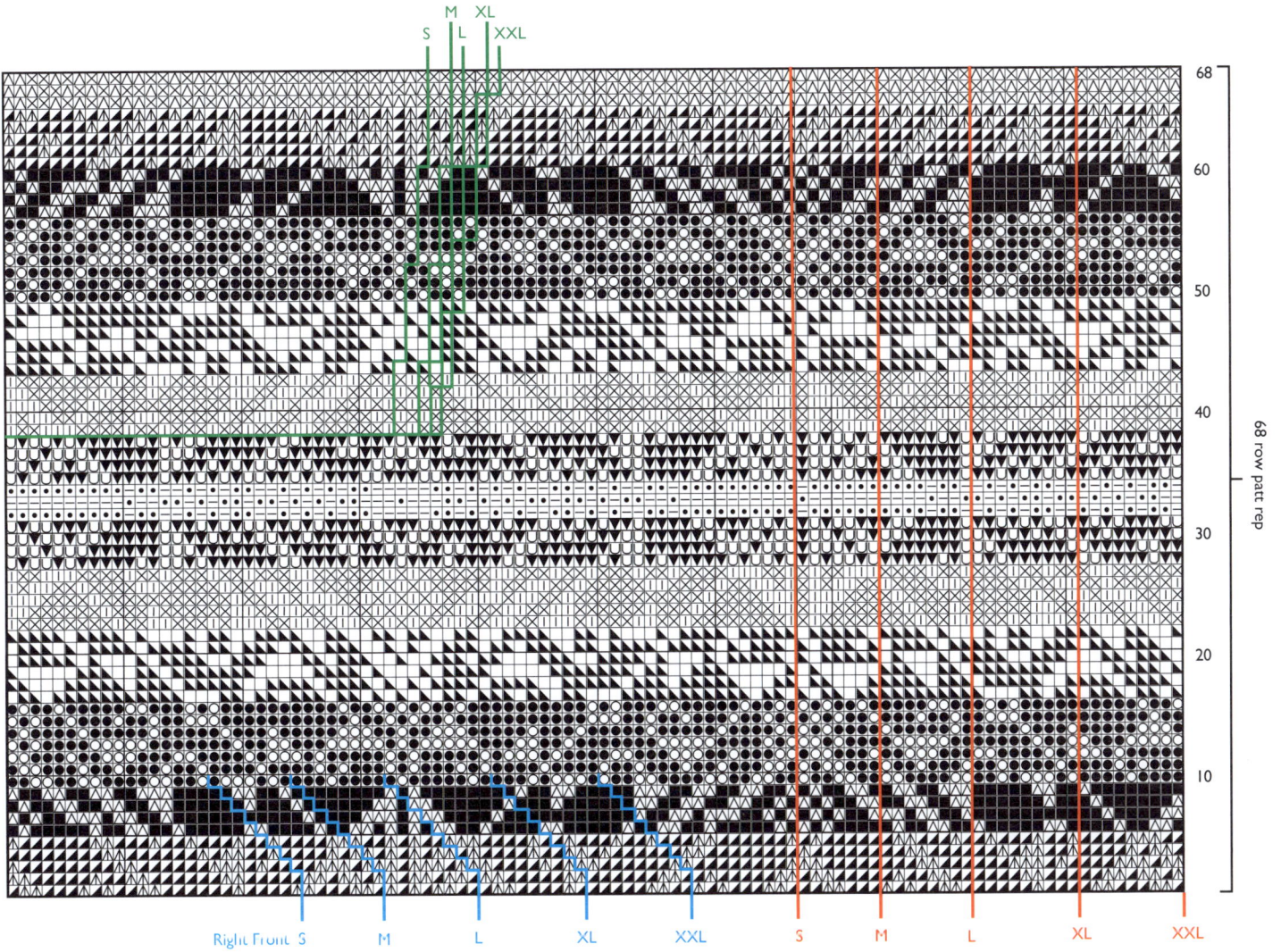

Right Front S   M   L   XL   XXL   S   M   L   XL   XXL

68

60

50

40

30

20

10

68 row patt rep

POPPY SCARF

● ●

Size
One size only

Marie Wallin British Breeds

A Woad	2	x 25gm
B Eau de Nil	2	x 25gm
C Chestnut	1	x 25gm
D Blossom	1	x 25gm
E Wood	2	x 25gm
F Pale Oak	2	x 25gm
G Russet	1	x 25gm
H Quince	1	x 25gm
I Mulberry	2	x 25gm
J Foxglove	2	x 25gm
K Dark Apple	1	x 25gm
L Lime Flower	1	x 25gm

Needles
3¼mm (no 10) (US 3) circular needle no more than 40 cm (16 in) long

Tension
28 sts and 29 rounds to 10 cm measured over patterned st st using 3¼mm (US 3) circular needle.

Finished size
Completed scarf measures 23.5 cm (9¼ in) wide and 126.5 cm (49¾ in) long.

SCARF
Using 3¼mm (US 3) circular needle and yarn A cast on 132 sts. Joining in and breaking off colours as required, using the **fairisle technique** as described on the information page and repeating the 66 st patt repeat twice around each round and repeating the 94 round patt repeat throughout, cont in patt from chart, which is worked entirely in st st (K every round), for 282 rounds (3 patt repeats), then work rounds 1 to 85 again. 367 rounds in total. Cast off.

MAKING UP
Press as described on the information page.
Sew in any loose ends on WS of scarf.
Smooth out the scarf so that it is flat and close the bottom and top edges by using mattress stitch.

KEY

- ■ A. Woad
- ✕ B. Eau de Nil
- ▼ C. Chestnut
- ○ D. Blossom
- ● E. Wood
- · F. Pale Oak
- ◢ G. Russet
- ∪ H. Quince
- ▲ I. Mulberry
- □ J. Foxglove
- ◣ K. Dark Apple
- ı L. Lime Flower

66 st patt rep

94 round patt rep

43.5 [43.5: 47: 47: 47] cm
(17 [17: 18½: 18½: 18½] in)

70 [71: 72: 73: 74] cm
(27½ [28: 28¼: 28¾: 29¼] in)

43 [50: 57: 64: 71] cm
(17 [19¾: 22½: 25¼: 28] in)

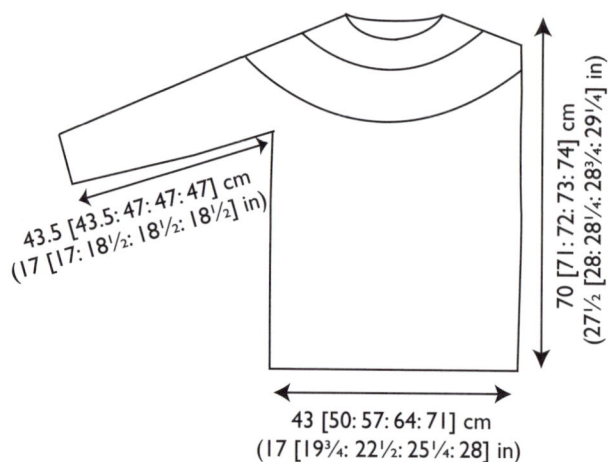

To fit bust	S	M	L	XL	XXL	
	81-86	91-97	102-107	112-117	122-127	cm
	32-34	36-38	40-42	44-46	48-50	in

Marie Wallin British Breeds

		S	M	L	XL	XXL	
A	Blossom	15	17	19	22	24	x 25gm
B	Mallard	1	1	1	1	1	x 25gm
C	Silver Birch	1	1	1	1	1	x 25gm
D	Russet	1	1	1	1	1	x 25gm
E	Quince	1	1	1	1	1	x 25gm
F	Dark Apple	1	1	1	1	1	x 25gm
G	Chestnut	1	1	1	1	1	x 25gm
H	Pale Oak	1	1	1	1	1	x 25gm
I	Wood	1	1	1	1	1	x 25gm
J	Eau de Nil	1	1	1	1	1	x 25gm
K	Rose	1	1	1	1	1	x 25gm
L	Foxglove	1	1	1	1	1	x 25gm

Needles

2¾mm (no 12) (US 2) circular needle
3¼mm (no 10) (US 3) circular needle
Set of 4 double-pointed 2¾mm (no 12) (US 2) needles
Set of 4 double-pointed 3¼mm (no 10) (US 3) needles

Tension

28 sts and 36 rounds to 10 cm measured over lace patt, 28 sts and 29 rounds to 10 cm measured over patterned st st, both using 3¼mm (US 3) circular needle. 28 sts and 36 rounds to 10 cm measured over plain st st using 2¾mm (US 2) circular needle.

SPECIAL ABBREVIATION

Tw2R = K2tog leaving sts on left needle, K first st again and slip both sts off left needle together; **Tw2L** = K into back of second st on left needle, K tog tbl first 2 sts on left needle and slip both sts off left needle together.

BODY (worked in one piece to armholes)
Using 2¾mm (US 2) circular needle and yarn A cast on 240 [280: 320: 360: 400] sts.
Taking care not to twist cast-on edge and placing a marker on first st of next round to denote beg and end of rounds, cont as folls:
Round 1 (RS): *(K1, P1) 9 times, Tw2R, P1, (K1, P1) 8 times, Tw2R, P1, rep from * to end.
Round 2: *(K1, P1) 9 times, K2, P1, (K1, P1) 8 times, K2, P1, rep from * to end.
These 2 rounds form fancy rib.
Cont in fancy rib until work meas 7 cm, ending after round 2.
Change to 3¼mm (US 3) circular needle.
Beg and ending rounds as indicated, repeating the 24 round patt repeat throughout and repeating the 40 st patt repeat 6 [7: 8: 9: 10] times around each round, cont in patt from chart for body as folls:
Work 132 rounds, ending after patt round 12.
Next round: K8 and slip these sts onto a holder,

K56 [66: 76: 86: 96] and slip these sts onto another holder (for left back), K9 and slip these 9 sts onto a safety pin (for left underarm), K111 [131: 151: 171: 191] and slip these sts onto another holder (for front), K9 and slip these 9 sts onto another safety pin (for right underarm), K rem 47 [57: 67: 77: 87] and slip these sts onto another holder (for right back).
Break yarn.
Slip 8 sts on holder at beg of round onto same holder as last set of sts so that there are 55 [65: 75: 85: 95] sts on right back holder.

SLEEVES
Using set of 4 double-pointed 2¾mm (US 2) needles and yarn A cast on 54 [56: 58: 58: 62] sts.
Distribute sts evenly over 3 of the 4 needles and, taking care not to twist cast-on edge and placing a marker on first st of next round (to denote sleeve "seam"), cont as folls:
Round 1 (RS): P0 [1: 0: 0: 0], (K1, P1) 8 [8: 9: 9: 10] times, Tw2R, P1, (K1, P1) 9 times, Tw2R, (P1, K1) 7 [8: 8: 8: 9] times, P1 [0: 1: 1: 1].
Round 2: P0 [1: 0: 0: 0], (K1, P1) 8 [8: 9: 9: 10] times, K2, P1, (K1, P1) 9 times, K2, (P1, K1) 7 [8: 8: 8: 9] times, P1 [0: 1: 1: 1].
These 2 rounds form fancy rib.
Cont in fancy rib until work meas 7 cm, ending after round 2.
Change to double-pointed 3¼mm (US 3) needles.
Beg and ending rounds as indicated and repeating the 24 round patt repeat throughout, cont in patt from chart for sleeve **beg with chart round 13 [13: 1: 1: 1]** as folls:
Work 3 rounds.
Next round: Inc in first st, patt to last st, inc in last st.
Working all increases as set by last round, inc 1 st at each end of 6th [6th: 6th: 5th: 5th] and every foll 6th [6th: 6th: 5th: 5th] round to 60 [76: 82: 78: 94] sts, then on every foll 7th [7th: 7th: 6th: 6th] round until there are 90 [94: 100: 106: 112] sts, taking inc sts into patt.
Work 11 rounds, ending after chart round 24.
Next round: K5 and slip these 5 sts onto a safety pin (for underarm), K81 [85: 91: 97: 103] and slip these sts onto another holder (for sleeve), K4 and slip these sts onto same safety pin as first 5 sts – 9 sts now on underarm safety pin.
Break yarn.

YOKE
With RS facing, using 2¾mm (US 2) circular needle and yarn A, K across sts on holders as folls: K across 56 [66: 76: 86: 96] sts on left back holder, K across 81 [85: 91: 97: 103] sts on left sleeve holder, K across 111 [131: 151: 171: 191] sts on front holder, K across 81 [85: 91: 97: 103] sts on right sleeve holder, then K across 55 [65: 75: 85: 95] sts on right back holder.
384 [432: 484: 536: 588] sts.
Place marker on first st – this is centre back st.
(**Note**: As the number of sts decreases and they will no longer fit comfortably on circular needle, change to double-pointed needles.)
Work in st st (K every round) for 15 [16: 17: 19: 20] rounds.
Next round: K10 [8: 14: 4: 18], (K2, K2tog, K5 [5: 4: 4: 4], sl 1, K1,

psso, K2) 28 [32: 38: 44: 46] times, K10 [8: 14: 4: 18].
328 [368: 408: 448: 496] sts.
Work in st st for 5 [5: 6: 6: 7] rounds.
Change to 3¼mm (US 3) circular needle.
Beg and ending rounds as indicated, using the **fairisle technique** as described on the information page and repeating the 8 st patt repeat 41 [46: 51: 56: 62] times around each round, cont in patt from chart for yoke, which is worked entirely in st st (K every round), as folls:
Work chart rounds 1 to 13.
Chart round 14: Using yarn F, K8 [8: 6: 4: 6], (K2, K2tog, K5 [3: 3: 3: 3], sl 1, K1, psso, K2) 24 [32: 36: 40: 44] times, K8 [8: 6: 4: 6]. 280 [304: 336: 368: 408] sts.
Now repeating the 8 st patt repeat 35 [38: 42: 46: 51] times around each round, work chart rounds 15 to 27.
Chart round 28: Using yarn F, K0 [8: 6: 4: 12], (K2 [2: 2: 2: 1], K2tog, K2 [1: 1: 1: 2], sl 1, K1, psso, K2 [2: 2: 2: 1]) 28 [32: 36: 40: 48] times, K0 [8: 6: 4: 12].
224 [240: 264: 288: 312] sts.
Now repeating the 8 st patt repeat 28 [30: 33: 36: 39] times around each round, work chart rounds 29 to 41.
Change to 2¾mm (US 2) circular needle.
Break off contrasts and complete yoke in st st using yarn A **only**.
Work 3 [4: 4: 5: 5] rounds.
Next round: K0 [8: 3: 15: 12], (K1, K2tog, K2 [1: 1: 0: 0], sl 1, K1, psso, K1) 28 [32: 37: 43: 48] times, K0 [8: 2: 15: 12].
168 [176: 190: 202: 216] sts.
Work 16 [16: 18: 19: 21] rounds.
Next round: K0 [8: 3: 15: 12], (K1 [0: 0: 0: 0], K2tog, K0 [1: 1: 0: 0], sl 1, K1, psso, K1 [0: 0: 0: 0]) 28 [32: 37: 43: 48] times, K0 [8: 2: 15: 12]. 112 [112: 116: 116: 120] sts.
Work 1 round.
Work neckband
Next round: *K1, P1, rep from * to end.
Rep last round 4 times more.
Cast off in rib.

MAKING UP
Press as described on the information page.
See information page for finishing instructions, joining both body and sleeve underarm seams by grafting tog each set of 9 sts left on safety pins.

YOKE CHART

8 st patt rep

BODY CHART

40 st patt rep

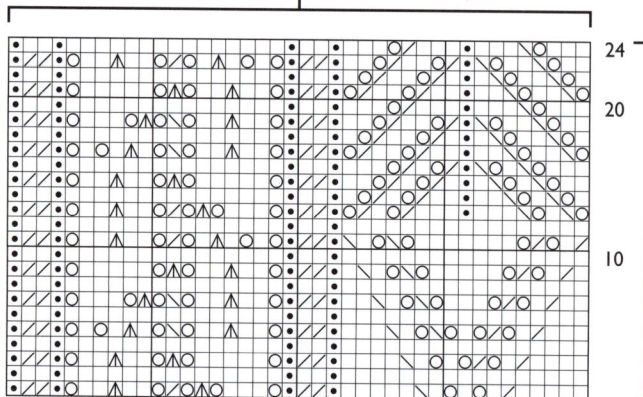

KEY

- ○ A. Blossom
- ▼ B. Mallard
- ∪ C. Silver Birch
- ◣ D. Russet
- □ E. Quince
- × F. Dark Apple
- ● G. Chestnut
- △ H. Pale Oak
- ■ I. Wood
- − J. Eau de Nil
- ◤ K. Rose
- ⋀ L. Foxglove

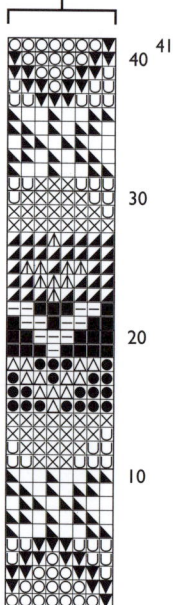

KEY

- □ Knit on RS, Purl on WS
- • Purl on RS, Knit on WS
- ╱ K2 tog on RS, P2 tog on WS
- ╲ Sl, K1, psso on RS, P2 tog tbl on WS
- ○ Yarn over
- ╱╱ Tw2R
- ╲╲ Tw2L
- ⋀ Sl 1, K2tog, psso

SLEEVE CHART

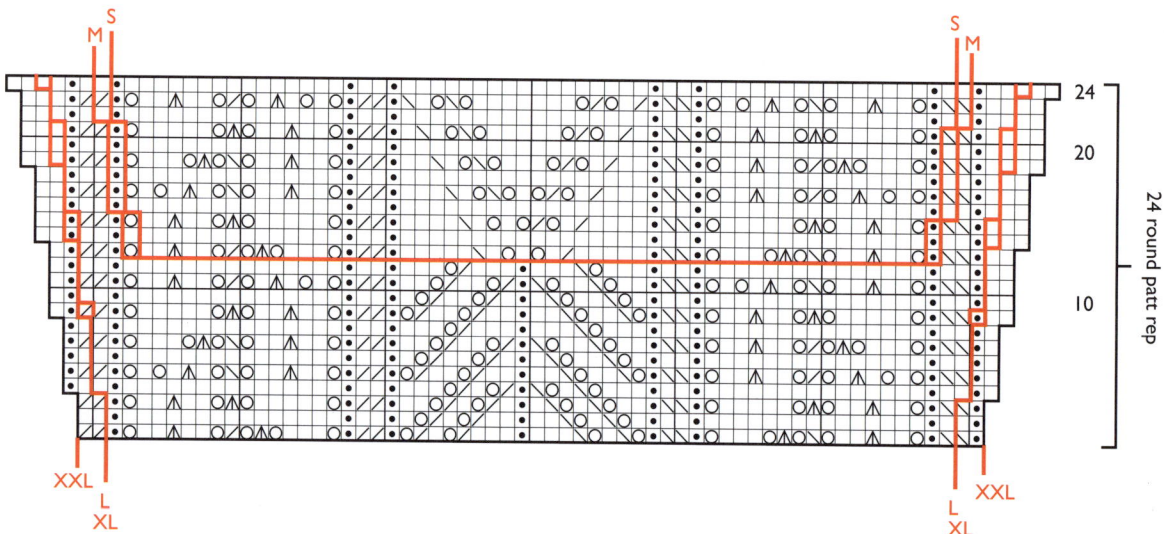

HONEYSUCKLE ● ● ●

56 [58: 60: 62: 64] cm
(22 [22¾: 23½: 24½: 25¼] in)

44 [45: 46: 46: 46] cm
(17¼ [17¾: 18: 18: 18] in)

47.5 [52.5: 59: 65.5: 72.5] cm
(18¾ [20¾: 23¼: 25¾: 28½] in)

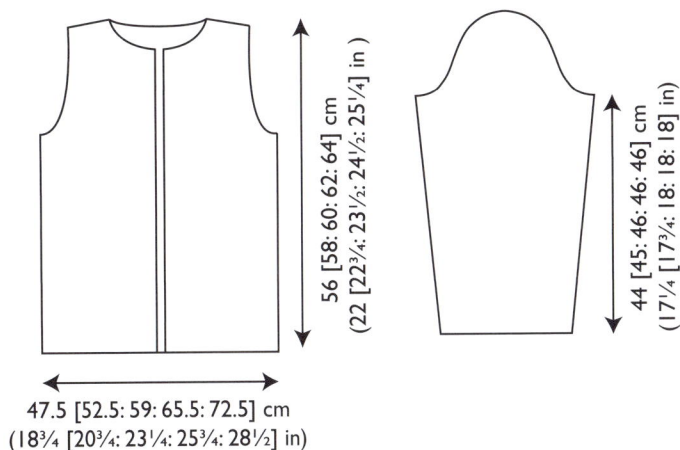

	S	M	L	XL	XXL	
To fit bust	81-86	91-97	102-107	112-117	122-127	cm
	32-34	36-38	40-42	44-46	48-50	in

Marie Wallin British Breeds

		S	M	L	XL	XXL	
A	Raw	4	4	5	5	6	x 25gm
B	Wood	2	2	3	3	3	x 25gm
C	Chestnut	2	2	2	2	2	x 25gm
D	Dark Apple	2	3	3	3	3	x 25gm
E	Mallard	3	3	3	4	4	x 25gm
F	Mulberry	3	3	4	4	4	x 25gm
G	Pale Oak	2	2	2	2	3	x 25gm
H	Quince	1	1	2	2	2	x 25gm
I	Foxglove	1	1	1	1	1	x 25gm
J	Lime Flower	1	1	2	2	2	x 25gm
K	Silver Birch	2	2	3	3	3	x 25gm

Needles
1 pair 2¾mm (no 12) (US 2) needles
1 pair 3¼mm (no 10) (US 3) needles

Buttons – 9 x TGB 1167 from Textile Garden – see information page for contact details.

Tension
28 sts and 29 rows to 10 cm measured over patterned st st using 3¼mm (US 3) needles.

BACK
Using 2¾mm (US 2) needles and yarn A cast on 133 [147: 165: 183: 203] sts.
Row 1 (RS): K1, *P1, K1, rep from * to end.
Joining in and breaking off colours as required and stranding yarn not in use across **WS** of work (this is front of work on WS rows, and back of work on RS rows), now work in striped 2 colour rib as folls:
Row 2 (WS): Using yarn A P1, *using yarn B K1, using yarn A P1, rep from * to end.
Row 3: Using yarn A K1, *using yarn B P1, using yarn A K1, rep from * to end.
Rows 4 and 5: As rows 2 and 3 **but** using yarn C instead of yarn B.
Rows 6 and 7: As rows 2 and 3 **but** using yarn D instead of yarn B.
Rows 8 and 9: As rows 2 and 3 **but** using yarn E instead of yarn B.
Rows 10 to 13: As rows 2 to 5.
Row 14: Using yarn A P1, *K1, P1, rep from * to end.
Change to 3¼mm (US 3) needles.
Beg and ending rows as indicated, using the **fairisle technique** as described on the information page and repeating the 74 row patt repeat throughout, cont in patt from chart, which is worked entirely in st st beg with a K row, as folls:
Cont straight until back meas 36 [37: 38: 39: 40] cm, ending with RS facing for next row.

Shape armholes

Keeping patt correct, cast off 6 [7: 8: 9: 10] sts at beg of next 2 rows. 121 [133: 149: 165: 183] sts.

Dec 1 st at each end of next 5 [7: 9: 11: 13] rows, then on foll 6 [7: 9: 11: 13] alt rows. 99 [105: 113: 121: 131] sts.

Cont straight until armhole meas 18 [19: 20: 21: 22] cm, ending with RS facing for next row.

Shape shoulders and back neck

Next row (RS): Cast off 5 [6: 7: 8: 9] sts, patt until there are 22 [24: 26: 29: 32] sts on right needle and turn, leaving rem sts on a holder.

Work each side of neck separately.

Dec 1 st at neck edge of next 4 rows **and at same time** cast off 6 [6: 7: 8: 9] sts at beg of 2nd row, then 6 [7: 7: 8: 9] sts at beg of foll alt row.

Work 1 row.

Cast off rem 6 [7: 8: 9: 10] sts.

With RS facing, slip centre 45 [45: 47: 47: 49] sts onto a holder (for neckband), rejoin yarns and patt to end.

Complete to match first side, reversing shapings.

LEFT FRONT

Using 2¾mm (US 2) needles and yarn A cast on 66 [72: 82: 90: 100] sts.

Row 1 (RS): K1, *P1, K1, rep from * to last st, K1.

Keeping yarn not in use at **WS** of work throughout (this is front of work on WS rows and back of work on RS rows), now work in striped 2 colour rib as folls:

Row 2 (WS): Using yarn A K1, P1, *using yarn B K1, using yarn A P1, rep from * to end.

Row 3: Using yarn A K1, *using yarn B P1, using yarn A K1, rep from * to last st, using yarn A K1.

Rows 4 and 5: As rows 2 and 3 **but** using yarn C instead of yarn B.

Rows 6 and 7: As rows 2 and 3 **but** using yarn D instead of yarn B.

Rows 8 and 9: As rows 2 and 3 **but** using yarn E instead of yarn B.

Rows 10 to 13: As rows 2 to 5.

Row 14: Using yarn A *K1, P1, rep from * to end, inc 0 [1: 0: 1: 0] st at end of row. 66 [73: 82: 91: 101] sts.

Change to 3¼mm (US 3) needles.

Beg and ending rows as indicated, cont in patt from chart as folls:

Cont straight until left front matches back to beg of armhole shaping, ending with RS facing for next row.

Shape armhole

Keeping patt correct, cast off 6 [7: 8: 9: 10] sts at beg of next row. 60 [66: 74: 82: 91] sts.

Work 1 row.

Dec 1 st at armhole edge of next 5 [7: 9: 11: 13] rows, then on foll 6 [7: 9: 11: 13] alt rows. 49 [52: 56: 60: 65] sts.

Cont straight until 18 [18: 20: 20: 22] rows less have been worked than on back to beg of shoulder shaping, ending with RS facing for next row.

Shape front neck

Next row (RS): Patt 35 [38: 42: 46: 51] sts and turn, leaving rem 14 sts on a holder (for neckband).

Keeping patt correct, dec 1 st at neck edge of next 8 rows, then

on foll 4 [4: 5: 5: 6] alt rows. 23 [26: 29: 33: 37] sts.

Work 1 row, ending with RS facing for next row.

Shape shoulder

Cast off 5 [6: 7: 8: 9] sts at beg of next and foll 0 [1: 2: 2: 2] alt rows, then 6 [7: -: -: -] sts at beg of foll 2 [1: -: -: -] alt rows.

Work 1 row.

Cast off rem 6 [7: 8: 9: 10] sts.

RIGHT FRONT

Using 2¾mm (US 2) needles and yarn A cast on 66 [72: 82: 90: 100] sts.

Row 1 (RS): K2, *P1, K1, rep from * to end.

Keeping yarn not in use at **WS** of work throughout (this is front of work on WS rows and back of work on RS rows), now work in striped 2 colour rib as folls:

Row 2 (WS): Using yarn A P1, *using yarn B K1, using yarn A P1, rep from * to last st, using yarn A K1.

Row 3: Using yarn A K2, *using yarn B P1, using yarn A K1, rep from * to end.

Rows 4 and 5: As rows 2 and 3 **but** using yarn C instead of yarn B.

Rows 6 and 7: As rows 2 and 3 **but** using yarn D instead of yarn B.

Rows 8 and 9: As rows 2 and 3 **but** using yarn E instead of yarn B.

Rows 10 to 13: As rows 2 to 5.

Row 14: Using yarn A (inc in first st) 0 [1: 0: 1: 1] time, P1 [0: 1: 0: 0], K1, *P1, K1, rep from * to end. 66 [73: 82: 91: 101] sts.

Change to 3¼mm (US 3) needles.

Beg and ending rows as indicated, cont in patt from chart and complete to match left front, reversing shapings and working first row of neck shaping as folls:

Shape front neck

Next row (RS): Break yarns. Slip first 14 sts onto a holder (for neckband). Rejoin yarns and patt to end. 35 [38: 42: 46: 51] sts.

SLEEVES

Using 2¾mm (US 2) needles and yarn A cast on 55 [59: 61: 61: 63] sts.

Work rib rows 1 to 14 as given for back.

Change to 3¼mm (US 3) needles.

Beg with chart row 51 [51: 49: 53: 55] and beg and ending rows as indicated, cont in patt from chart as folls:

Inc 1 st at each end of 3rd and every foll 4th row to 81 [83: 87: 99: 107] sts, then on every foll 6th row until there are 99 [103: 107: 111: 115] sts, taking inc sts into patt.

Cont straight until sleeve meas approx 44 [45: 46: 46: 46] cm, ending after same chart row as on back to beg of armhole shaping and with RS facing for next row.

Shape top

Keeping patt correct, cast off 6 [7: 8: 9: 10] sts at beg of next 2 rows. 87 [89: 91: 93: 95] sts.

Dec 1 st at each end of next 5 rows, then on every foll alt row until 53 sts rem, then on foll 11 rows, ending with RS facing for

next row. 31 sts.
Cast off 5 sts at beg of next 2 rows.
Cast off rem 21 sts.

MAKING UP
Press as described on the information page.
Join both shoulder seams using back stitch, or mattress stitch if preferred.

Neckband
With RS facing, using 2¾mm (US 2) needles and yarn A, K across 14 sts on right front holder, pick up and knit 25 [25: 27: 27: 29] sts up right side of front neck, and 5 sts down right side of back neck, K across 45 [45: 47: 47: 49] sts on back holder, pick up and knit 5 sts up left side of back neck, and 25 [25: 27: 27: 29] sts down left side of front neck, then K across 14 sts on left front holder. 133 [133: 139: 139: 145] sts.
**Row 1 (WS): K1, *P1, K1, rep from * to end.
Join in yarn D.
Keeping yarn not in use at **WS** of work throughout (this is front of work on WS rows and back of work on RS rows), cont as folls:
Row 2: Using yarn A K2, *using yarn D P1, using yarn A K1, rep from * to last st, using yarn A K1.
Row 3: Using yarn A K1, P1, *using yarn D K1, using yarn A P1, rep from * to last st, using yarn A K1.
Rep last 2 rows once more, ending with RS facing for next row.
Break off yarn D and cont using yarn A **only**.
Row 6 (RS): K2, *P1, K1, rep from * to last st, K1.
Cast off in rib (on **WS**).

Button band
With RS facing, using 2¾mm (US 2) needles and yarn A, pick up and knit 145 [153: 153: 161: 161] sts evenly down left front opening edge, from top of neckband to cast-on edge.
Complete as given for neckband from **.

Buttonhole band
Work to match button band, picking up sts evenly up right front opening edge and making 9 buttonholes in row 3 as folls:
Row 3 (WS): Rib 4, *yrn, work 2 tog (to make a buttonhole), rib 15 [16: 16: 17: 17], rep from * 7 times more, yrn, work 2 tog (to make 9th buttonhole), rib 3.
Join side seams. Join sleeve seams. Insert sleeves into armholes.
Sew on buttons.

KEY

A. ☐ Raw   D. ▲ Dark Apple   G. ╱ Pale Oak   J. • Lime Flower

B. ■ Wood   E. ◢ Mallard   H. ○ Quince   K. ✕ Silver Birch

C. ▮ Chestnut   F. ● Mulberry   I. ⋀ Foxglove

Sleeves

M
XL
L
XXL   S

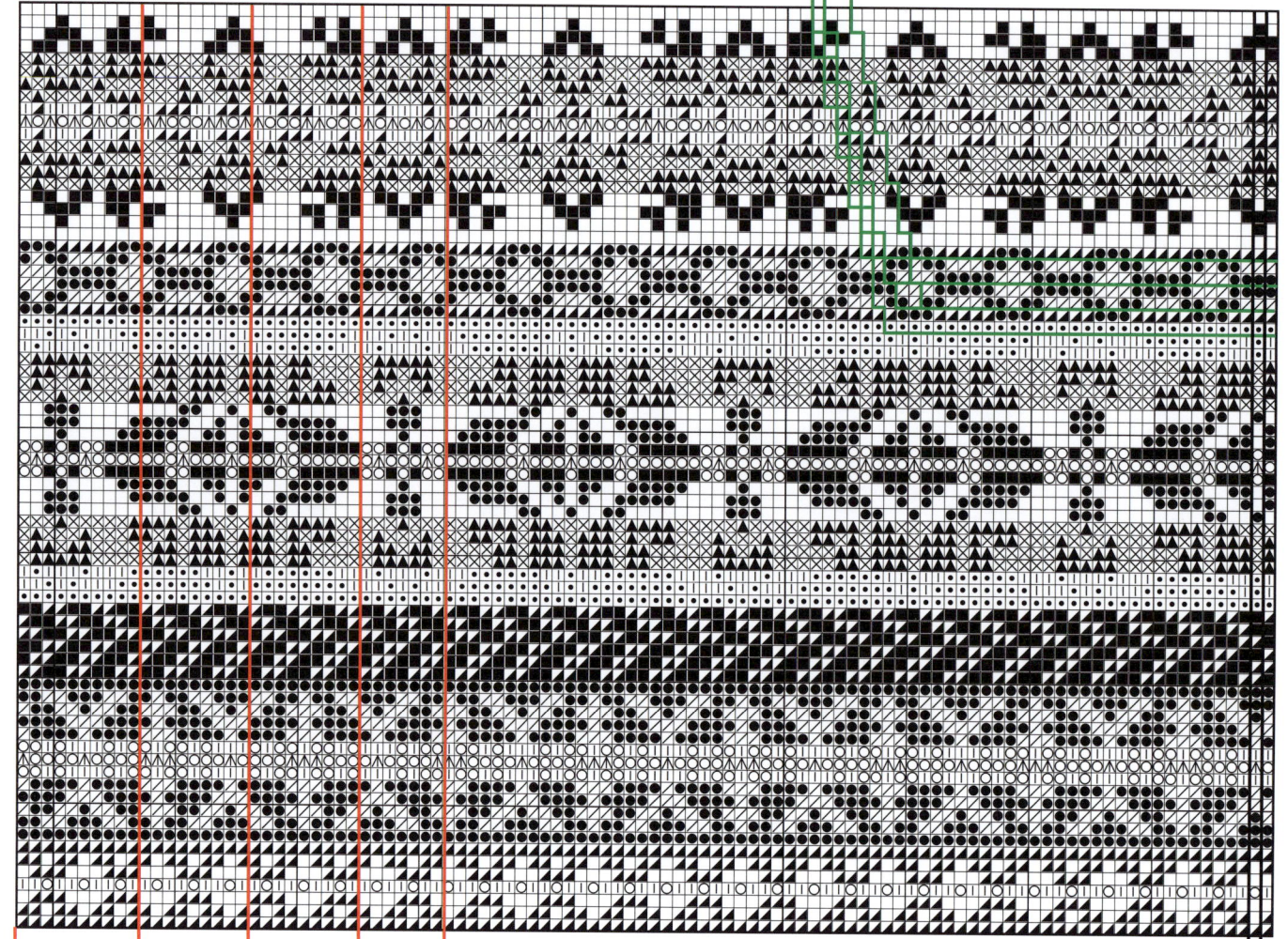

XXL   XL   L   M   S

Left

Right Front

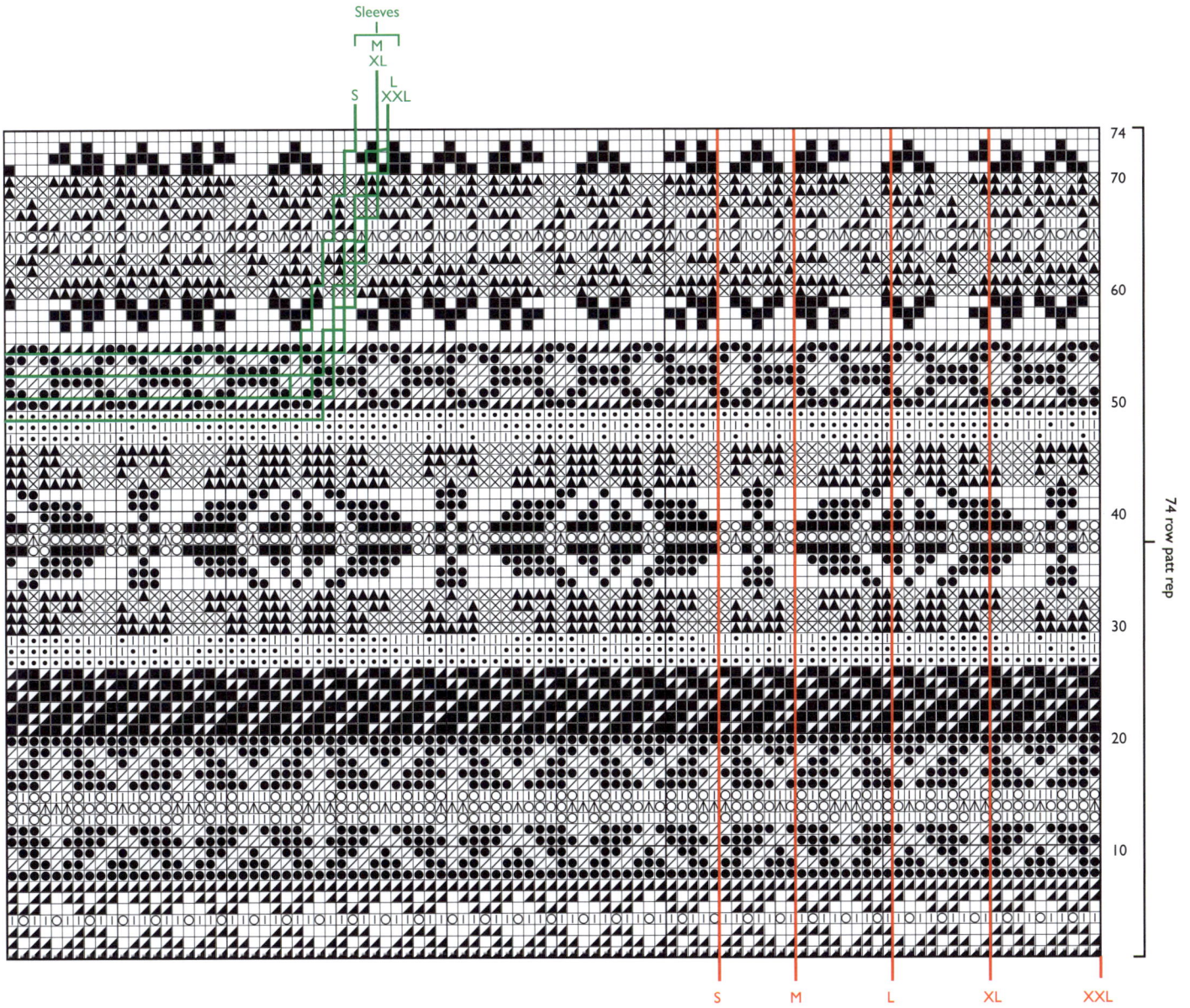

Sleeves

S M L
   XL XXL

74 row patt rep

S   M   L   XL   XXL

MISTLETOE TAM ● ●

One size only
To fit average head
53 – 56cm (21 – 22in)

Marie Wallin British Breeds

A	Raw	1	x 25gm
B	Wood	1	x 25gm
C	Blossom	1	x 25gm
D	Dark Apple	1	x 25gm
E	Lime Flower	1	x 25gm
F	Mallard	1	x 25gm
G	Silver Birch	1	x 25gm
H	Russet	1	x 25gm
I	Eau de Nil	1	x 25gm
J	Quince	1	x 25gm
K	Foxglove	1	x 25gm

Needles
2¾mm (no 12) (US 2) circular needle or set of 4 double-pointed
2¾mm (no 12) (US 2) needles
3¼mm (no 10) (US 3) circular needle or set of 4 double-pointed
3¼mm (no 10) (US 3) needles

Tension
28 sts and 29 rounds to 10 cm measured over patterned st st using 3¼mm (US 3) needles.

TAM
Brim
Using 2¾mm (US 2) circular needle or double-pointed needles and yarn A cast on 114 sts.
Taking care not to twist cast-on edge, work in rounds as folls:
Round 1 (RS): *K1, P1, rep from * to end.
Place marker on first st of round just knitted to denote beg and end of rounds.
Join in yarn H.
Keeping yarn not in use at **WS** of work, cont as folls:
Round 2: *Using yarn A K1, using yarn H P1, rep from * to end.
Rep round 2, 3 times more, Break off yarn H and cont in yarn A **only**.
Next round: *K1, P1, rep from * to end.
Next round: K2tog, K to last 2 sts, K2tog. 112 sts.
Break off yarn A.
Change to 3¼mm (US 3) circular needle or double-pointed needles.
Join in yarn B.
Increase round: Using yarn B, K1, *M1, K2, rep from * to last st, M1, K1. 168 sts.
Work sides and crown of tam
Joining in and breaking off colours as required and using the **fairisle technique** as described on the information page, work from chart, which is worked entirely in st st (K every round) as folls:
Beg with **round 2** of chart, work the first 12 sts of chart, rep

the 24 st patt repeat 6 times, then work the last 12 sts of chart on each round until round 62 has been completed, working decreases as indicated on the following rounds:

Round 41: (Patt 10 sts, sl 1, K2tog, psso, patt 11 sts) 7 times. 154 sts.

Round 43: (Patt 9 sts, sl 1, K2tog, psso, patt 10 sts) 7 times. 140 sts.

Round 45: (Patt 8 sts, sl 1, K2tog, psso, patt 9 sts) 7 times. 126 sts.

Round 47: (Patt 7 sts, sl 1, K2tog, psso, patt 8 sts) 7 times. 112 sts.

Round 49: (Patt 6 sts, sl 1, K2tog, psso, patt 7 sts) 7 times. 98 sts.

Round 51: (Patt 5 sts, sl 1, K2tog, psso, patt 6 sts) 7 times. 84 sts.

Round 53: (Patt 4 sts, sl 1, K2tog, psso, patt 5 sts) 7 times. 70 sts.

Round 55: (Patt 3 sts, sl 1, K2tog, psso, patt 4 sts) 7 times. 56 sts.

Round 57: (Patt 2 sts, sl 1, K2tog, psso, patt 3 sts) 7 times. 42 sts.

Cont in yarn A **only** as folls:

Round 59: (K1, sl 1, K2tog, psso, K2) 7 times. 28 sts.

Round 61: (sl 1, K2tog, psso, K1) 7 times. 14 sts.

Round 62: (K2tog) 7 times. 7 sts.

Break off yarn, thread through rem sts and draw up tightly.

FINISHING

Fasten off centre of tam on WS.

Weave in any loose ends on WS of tam.

Press tam gently on WS using a warm iron over a damp cloth.

KEY

☐ A. Raw

■ B. Wood

• C. Blossom

● D. Dark Apple

| E. Lime Flower

▲ F. Mallard

✕ G. Silver Birch

◤ H. Russet

○ I. Eau de Nil

╱ J. Quince

∪ K. Foxglove

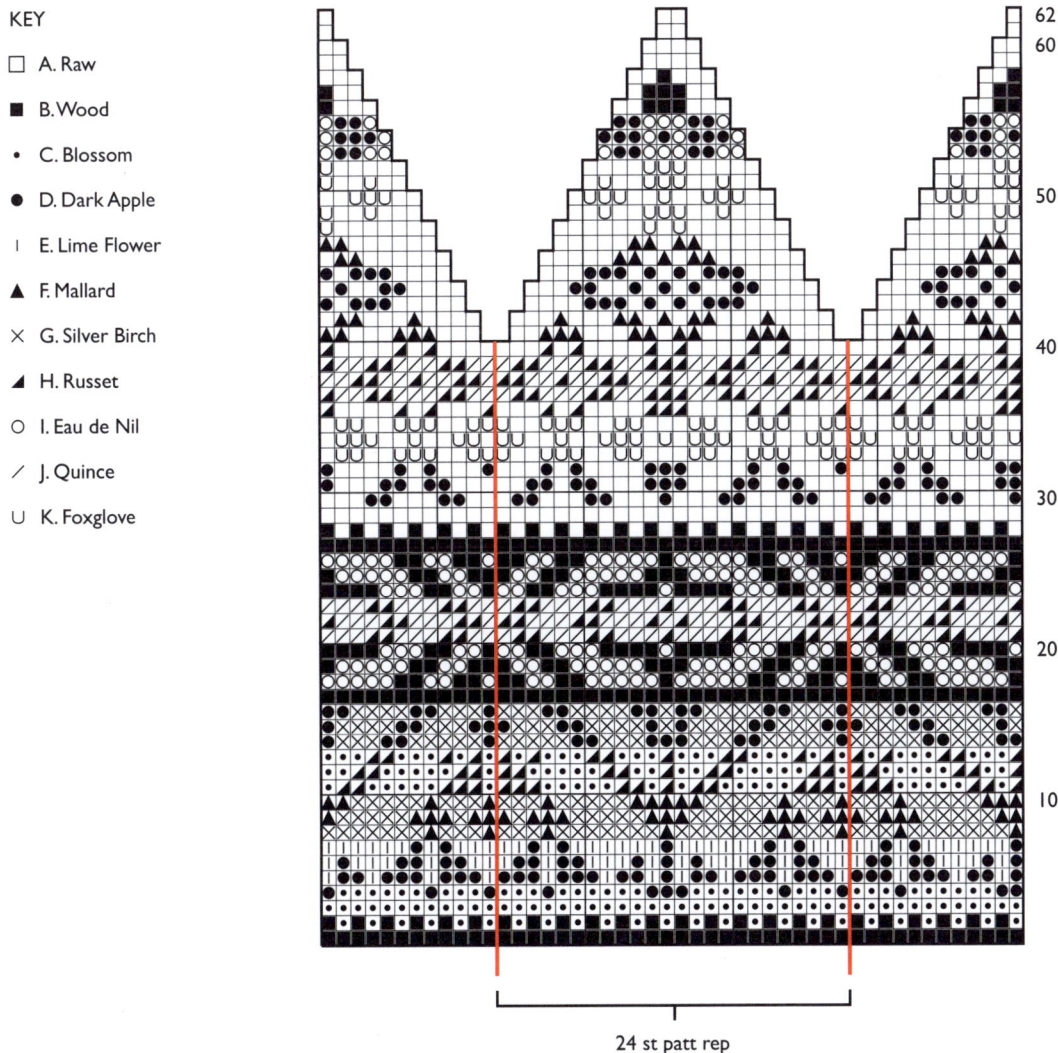

24 st patt rep

IVY

● ● ●

53 [55: 57: 59: 61] cm
(20¾ [21¼: 22½: 23¼: 24] in)

30 [31: 32: 32: 32] cm
(11¾ [12¼: 12½: 12½: 12½] in)

53 [56.5: 61: 69: 74] cm
(20¾ [22¼: 24: 27¼: 29¼] in)

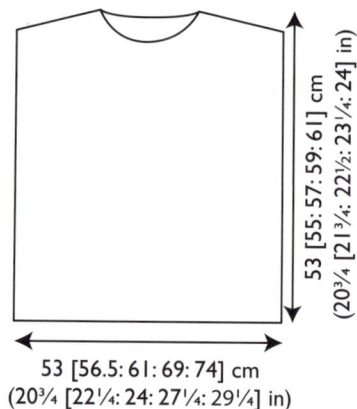

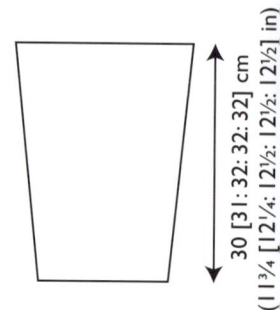

	S	M	L	XL	XXL	
To fit bust	81-86	91-97	102-107	112-117	122-127	cm
	32-34	36-38	40-42	44-46	48-50	in

Marie Wallin British Breeds

	18	20	22	25	27	x 25gm

(photographed in Silver Birch)

Needles

1 pair 2¾mm (no 12) (US 2) knitting needles
1 pair 3¼mm (no 10) (US 3) knitting needles
Cable needle

Tension

37 sts and 34 rows to 10 cm measured over sleeve and side body patt using 3¼mm (US 3) knitting needles. Central panel (88 sts) measures 22 cm.

SPECIAL ABBREVIATIONS

C4B = slip next 2 sts onto cable needle and leave at back of work, K2, then K2 from cable needle; **C4F** = slip next 2 sts onto cable needle and leave at front of work, K2, then K2 from cable needle; **Cr4L** = slip next 2 sts onto cable needle and leave at front of work, P2, then K2 from cable needle; **Cr4R** = slip next 2 sts onto cable needle and leave at back of work, K2, then P2 from cable needle; **Tw2R** = K2tog leaving sts on left needle, K first st again and slip both sts off left needle together; **Tw2L** = K into back of second st on left needle, K tog tbl first 2 sts on left needle

and slip both sts off left needle together.

PATTERN NOTE

Right rows are worked on 'even numbered' chart rows and wrong side rows on 'odd numbered' chart rows.

BACK
Using 2¾mm (US 2) needles cast on 202 [216: 232: 262: 280] sts.
Noting that row 1 is a **WS** row, beg and ending rows as indicated and repeating the side 26 st patt repeats 2 [2: 2: 3: 3] times at each side of central sts, cont in patt from chart for body as folls:
Work chart rows 1 to 4, 7 times, ending with **WS** facing for next row.
Change to 3¼mm (US 3) needles.
Work chart rows 5 to 54, ending with **WS** facing for next row.
Now repeating the 26 row patt repeat over centre sts (chart rows 55 to 80) and 20 row patt repeat over side sts (chart rows 55 to 74), cont as folls:
Cont straight until back meas 49 [51: 53: 55: 57] cm, ending with RS facing for next row.
Shape shoulders
Keeping patt correct, cast off 5 [6: 7: 8: 9] sts at beg of next 6 [12: 12: 10: 12] rows, then 6 [-: -: 9: -] sts at beg of foll 6 [-: -: 2: -] rows. 136 [144: 148: 164: 172] sts.
Shape back neck
Next row (RS): Cast off 6 [7: 7: 9: 9] sts, patt until there are 23 [26: 26: 32: 34] sts on right needle and turn, leaving rem sts on a holder.
Work each side of neck separately.

Keeping patt correct, dec 1 st at neck edge of next 5 rows, ending with RS facing for next row, **and at same time** cast off 6 [7: 7: 9: 9] sts at beg of 2nd row, then 6 [7: 7: 9: 10] sts at beg of foll alt row.
Cast off rem 6 [7: 7: 9: 10] sts.
With RS facing, slip centre 78 [78: 82: 82: 86] sts onto a holder (for neckband), rejoin yarn and patt to end.
Complete to match first side, reversing shapings.

FRONT
Work as given for back until 2 [2: 6: 6: 10] rows less have been worked than on back to beg of shoulder shaping, ending with RS facing for next row.
Shape front neck
Next row (RS): Patt 71 [78: 86: 101: 110] sts and turn, leaving rem sts on a holder.
Work each side of neck separately.
Keeping patt correct, dec 1 st at neck edge of next 1 [1: 5: 5: 9] rows, ending with RS facing for next row. 70 [77: 81: 96: 101] sts.
Shape shoulder
Keeping patt correct, cast off 5 [6: 7: 8: 9] sts at beg of next and foll 2 [5: 8: 4: 7] alt rows, then 6 [7: -: 9: 10] sts at beg of foll 6 [3: -: 4: 1] alt rows **and at same time** dec 1 st at neck edge of next 9 [9: 5: 5: 1] rows, then on foll 4 [4: 6: 6: 8] alt rows.
Work 1 row.
Cast off rem 6 [7: 7: 9: 10] sts.
With RS facing, slip centre 60 sts onto a holder (for neckband), rejoin yarn and patt to end.
Complete to match first side, reversing shapings.

SLEEVES
Using 2¾mm (US 2) needles cast on 104 [108: 112: 112: 114] sts.
Noting that row 1 is a **WS** row, beg and ending rows as indicated and repeating the 26 st patt repeat 3 times across each row, cont in patt from chart for sleeve as folls:
Work chart rows 1 to 4, 7 times, ending with **WS** facing for next row.

Change to 3¼mm (US 3) needles.
Now repeating chart rows 5 to 24 **throughout** and noting that all sleeve increases will be on WS rows, cont as folls:
Inc 1 st at each end of 3rd [3rd: 3rd: next: next] and every foll 6th [4th: 4th: alt: alt] row to 124 [118: 132: 120: 130] sts, then on every foll – [6th: 6th: 4th: 4th] row until there are 124 [132: 140: 148: 154] sts, taking inc sts into patt.
Cont straight until sleeve meas 30 [31: 32: 32: 32] cm, ending with RS facing for next row.
Cast off.

MAKING UP
Press as described on the information page.
Join right shoulder seam using back stitch, or mattress stitch if preferred.
Neckband
With RS facing and using 2¾mm (US 2) needles, pick up and knit 20 [20: 23: 23: 26] sts down left side of front neck, K across 60 sts on front holder as folls: (K1, K2tog, K1) 15 times, pick up and knit 20 [20: 23: 23: 26] sts up right side of front neck, and 5 sts down right side of back neck, K across 78 [78: 82: 82: 86] sts on back holder as folls: K3 [3: 1: 1: 3], (K1, K2tog, K1) 18 [18: 20: 20: 20] times, K3 [3: 1: 1: 3], then pick up and knit 5 sts up left side of back neck. 155 [155: 163: 163: 173] sts.
Row 1 (WS): P1, *K1, P1, rep from * to end.
Row 2: K1, *P1, K1, rep from * to end.
Last 2 rows form rib.
Work in rib for a further 3 rows, ending with RS facing for next row.
Cast off in rib.
Join left shoulder and neckband seam. Mark points along side seam edges 18 [19: 20: 21: 22] cm either side of shoulder seams (to denote base of armhole openings). See information page for finishing instructions, setting in sleeves using the straight cast-off method.

Rep these 26 sts, 3 times

SLEEVE CHART

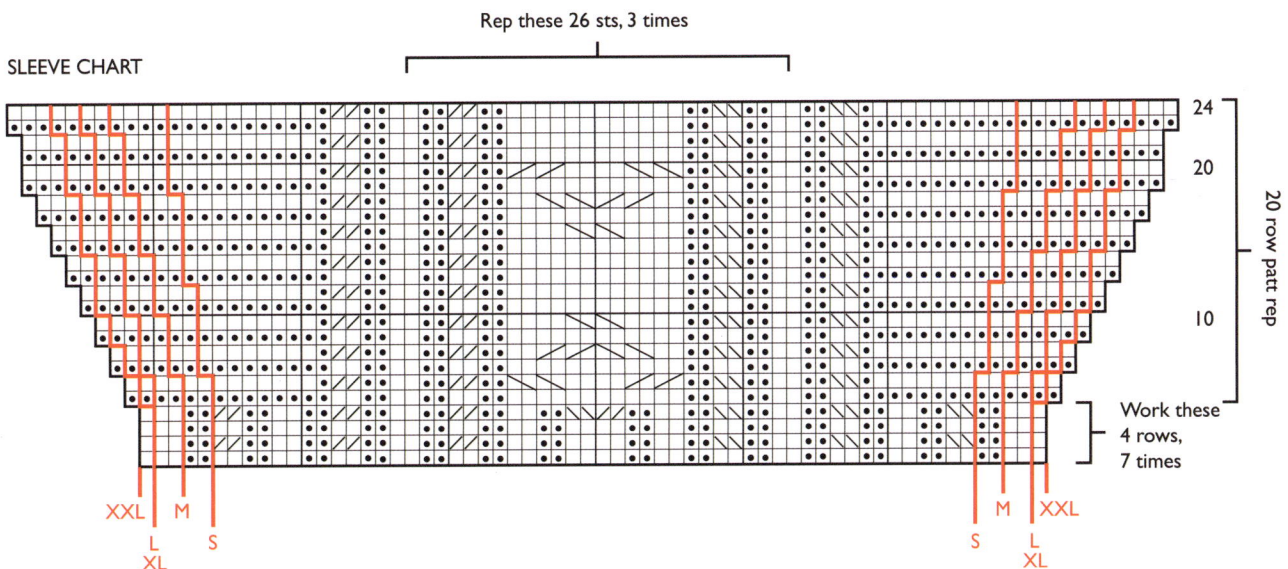

XXL M
L S
XL

S M XXL
L
XL

24
20
10

20 row patt rep

Work these 4 rows, 7 times

KEY

☐ Knit on RS, Purl on WS   • Purl on RS, Knit on WS   ⬚ Tw2R   ⬚ Tw2L   ⬚ C4B   ⬚ C4F   ⬚ Cr4R   ⬚ Cr4L

BODY CHART

20 row patt rep

Rep these 26 sts 2 [2: 2: 3: 3] times

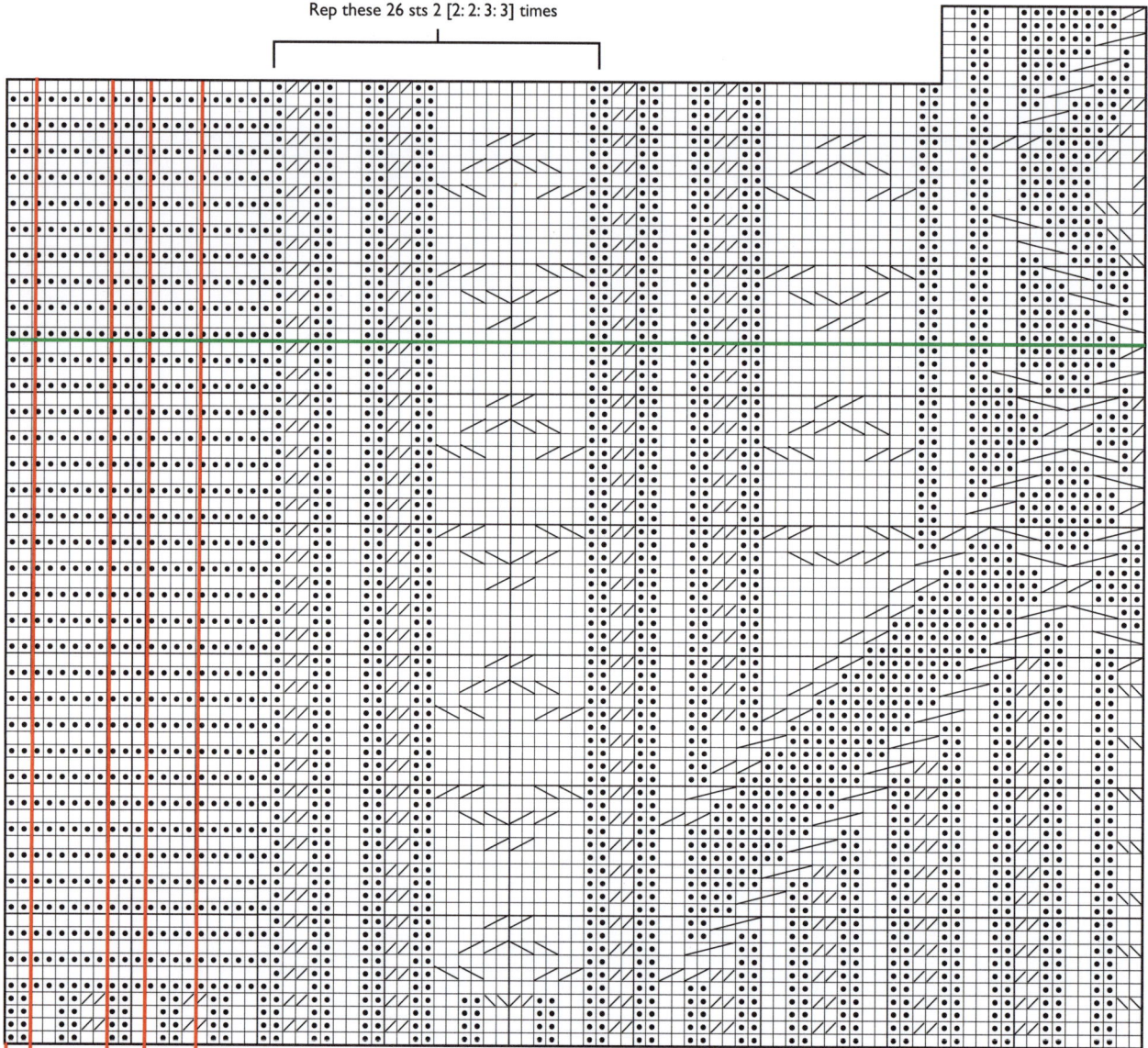

L   XXL   M   XL   S

26 row patt rep

20 row patt rep

80

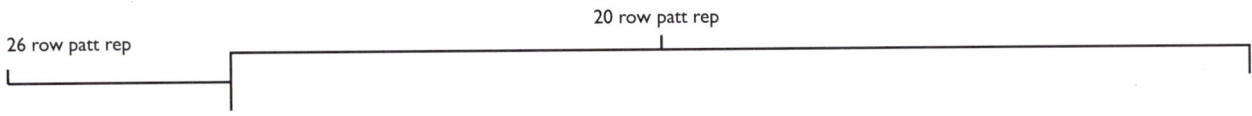

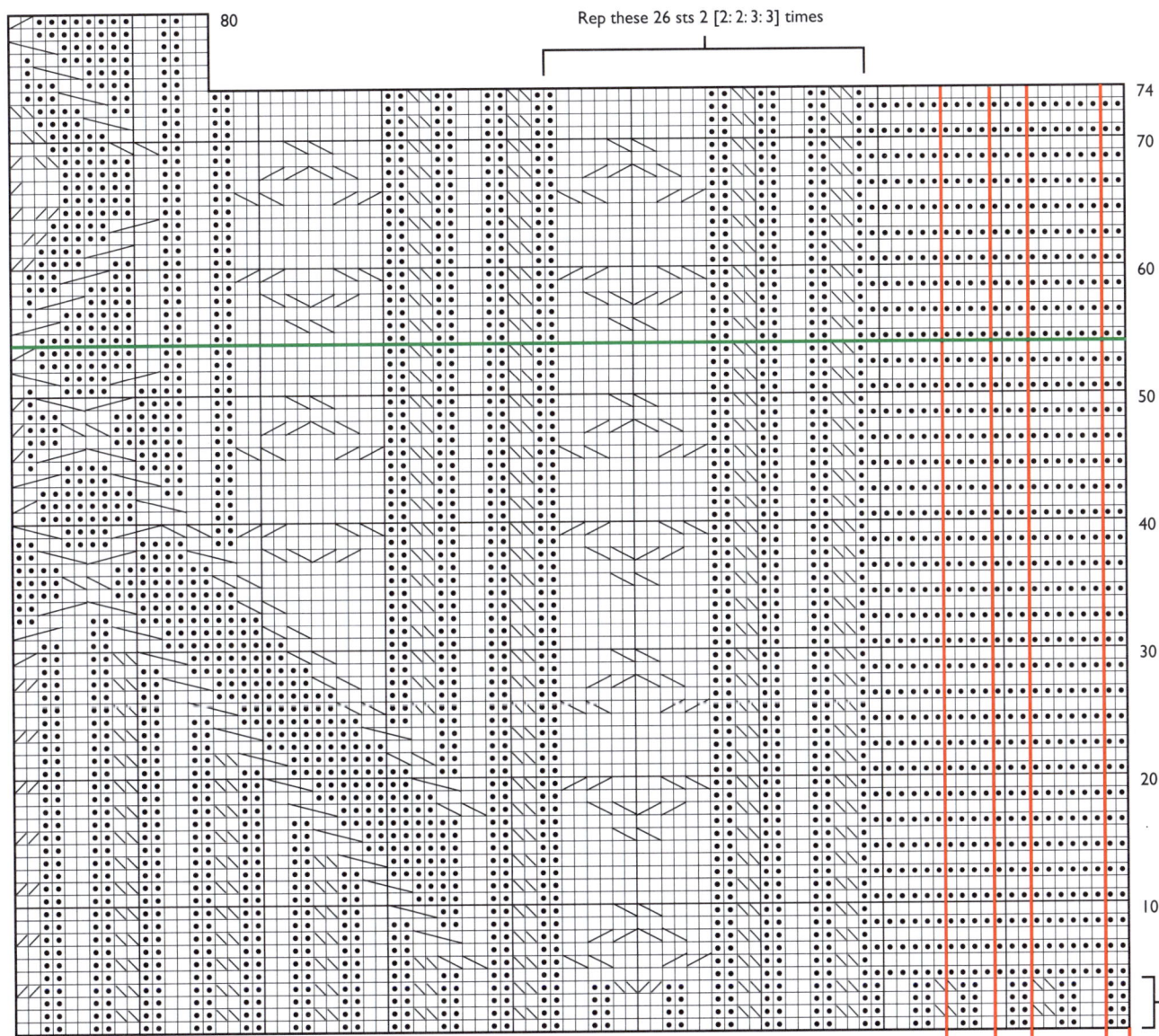

Rep these 26 sts 2 [2: 2: 3: 3] times

74

70

60

50

40

30

20

10

Work these
4 rows,
7 times

S   XL M   XXL L

BRAMBLE ● ● ●

Schematic measurements:
54 [56: 58: 60: 62] cm (21¼ [22: 22¾: 23½: 24½] in)

44 [49: 55.5: 61: 68] cm
(17¼ [19¼: 21¾: 24: 26¾] in)

44 [45: 46: 46: 46] cm (17¾ [17¾: 18: 18] in)

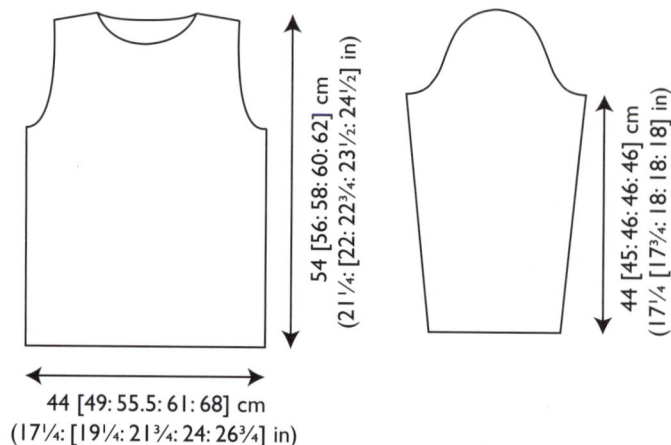

To fit bust	S	M	L	XL	XXL	
	81-86	91-97	102-107	112-117	122-127	cm
	32-34	36-38	40-42	44-46	48-50	in

Marie Wallin British Breeds

		S	M	L	XL	XXL	
A	Silver Birch	3	4	4	4	5	x 25gm
B	Mallard	1	1	1	1	2	x 25gm
C	Rose	2	2	2	2	2	x 25gm
D	Eau de Nil	2	3	3	3	4	x 25gm
E	Wood	2	3	3	3	3	x 25gm
F	Dark Apple	2	2	2	2	2	x 25gm
G	Quince	3	3	3	3	4	x 25gm
H	Russet	1	2	2	2	2	x 25gm
I	Foxglove	1	1	2	2	2	x 25gm
J	Pale Oak	2	2	2	3	3	x 25gm
K	Chestnut	2	2	2	2	2	x 25gm
L	Lime Flower	1	1	1	1	2	x 25gm

Needles

1 pair 2¾mm (no 12) (US 2) knitting needles
1 pair 3¼mm (no 10) (US 3) knitting needles

Tension

28 sts and 29 rows to 10 cm measured over patterned st st using 3¼mm (US 3) needles.

BACK

Using 2¾mm (US 2) needles and yarn A cast on 123 [137: 155: 171: 191] sts.
**Row 1 (RS): K1, *P1, K1, rep from * to end.
Joining in and breaking off colours as required and stranding yarn not in use across **WS** of work (this is front on WS rows, and back on RS rows), cont as folls:
Row 2: Using yarn A P1, *using yarn B K1, using yarn A P1, rep from * to end.
Row 3: Using yarn A K1, *using yarn B P1, using yarn A K1, rep from * to end.
Rows 4 and 5: As rows 2 and 3 but using yarn F in place of yarn B.
Rows 6 and 7: As rows 2 and 3 but using yarn K in place of yarn B.
Rows 8 and 9: As rows 2 and 3 but using yarn C in place of yarn B.
Rep last 8 rows once more.
Row 18 (WS): Using yarn A P1, *K1, P1, rep from * to end.
Row 19: Using yarn A K1, *P1, K1, rep from * to end.
Change to 3¼mm (US 3) needles.**
Beg and ending rows as indicated, using the **fairisle technique** as described on the information page and repeating the 66 row patt repeat throughout, cont in patt from chart for body, which is worked entirely in st st beg with a **purl** row, as folls:
Cont straight until back meas 34 [35: 36: 37: 38] cm, ending with RS facing for next row.
Shape armholes
Keeping patt correct, cast off 6 [7: 8: 9: 10] sts at beg of next 2 rows. 111 [123: 139: 153: 171] sts.

Dec 1 st at each end of next 5 [7: 9: 11: 13] rows, then on foll 2 [3: 5: 6: 8] alt rows, then on foll 4th row. 95 [101: 109: 117: 127] sts.
Cont straight until armhole meas 18 [19: 20: 21: 22] cm, ending with RS facing for next row.

Shape shoulders and back neck
Next row (RS): Cast off 5 [6: 7: 8: 9] sts, patt until there are 21 [23: 25: 28: 31] sts on right needle and turn, leaving rem sts on a holder.
Work each side of neck separately.
Keeping patt correct, dec 1 st at neck edge of next 4 rows **and at same time** cast off 5 [6: 7: 8: 9] sts at beg of 2nd row, then 6 [6: 7: 8: 9] sts at beg of foll alt row.
Work 1 row.
Cast off rem 6 [7: 7: 8: 9] sts.
With RS facing, slip centre 43 [43: 45: 45: 47] sts onto a holder (for neckband), rejoin yarns and patt to end.
Complete to match first side, reversing shapings.

FRONT
Work as given for back until 18 [18: 20: 20: 22] rows less have been worked than on back to beg of shoulder shaping, ending with RS facing for next row.

Shape front neck
Next row (RS): Patt 32 [35: 39: 43: 48] sts and turn, leaving rem sts on a holder.
Work each side of neck separately.
Keeping patt correct, dec 1 st at neck edge of next 6 rows, then on foll 3 [3: 4: 4: 5] alt rows, then on foll 4th row.
22 [25: 28: 32: 36] sts.
Work 1 row, ending with RS facing for next row.

Shape shoulder
Cast off 5 [6: 7: 8: 9] sts at beg of next and foll 1 [2: 2: 2: 2] alt rows, then 6 [-: -: -: -] sts at beg of foll 1 [-: -: -: -] alt row.
Work 1 row.
Cast off rem 6 [7: 7: 8: 9] sts.
With RS facing, slip centre 31 sts onto a holder (for neckband), rejoin yarns and patt to end.
Complete to match first side, reversing shapings.

SLEEVES
Using 2¾mm (US 2) needles and yarn A cast on 53 [57: 59: 59: 61] sts.
Work as given for back from ** to **.
Beg and ending rows as indicated, using the **fairisle technique** as described on the information page and repeating the 42 row patt repeat throughout, cont in patt from chart for sleeve, which is worked entirely in st st beg with a **purl** row, as folls:
Inc 1 st at each end of 2nd and every foll 4th row to 81 [81: 87: 99: 107] sts, then on every foll 6th row until there are 95 [99: 103: 107: 111] sts, taking inc sts into patt.
Cont straight until sleeve meas 44 [45: 46: 46: 46] cm, ending with RS facing for next row.

Shape top
Keeping patt correct, cast off 6 [7: 8: 9: 10] sts at beg of next 2 rows. 83 [85: 87: 89: 91] sts.

Dec 1 st at each end of next 7 rows, then on every foll alt row until 57 sts rem, then on foll 9 rows, ending with RS facing for next row. 39 sts.
Cast off 4 sts at beg of next 4 rows.
Cast off rem 23 sts.

MAKING UP
Press as described on the information page.
Join right shoulder seam using back stitch, or mattress stitch if preferred.

Neckband
With RS facing, using 2¾mm (US 2) needles and yarn A, pick up and knit 25 [25: 27: 27: 29] sts down left side of front neck, K across 31 sts on front holder, pick up and knit 25 [25: 27: 27: 29] sts up right side of front neck, and 5 sts down right side of back neck, K across 43 [43: 45: 45: 47] sts on back holder dec 1 st at centre, then pick up and knit 5 sts up left side of back neck.
133 [133: 139: 139: 145] sts.
Row 1 (WS): P1, *K1, P1, rep from * to end.
Joining in and breaking off colours as required and stranding yarn not in use across **WS** of work (this is front on WS rows, and back on RS rows), cont as folls:
Row 2: Using yarn A K1, *using yarn B P1, using yarn A K1, rep from * to end.
Row 3: Using yarn A P1, *using yarn B K1, using yarn A P1, rep from * to end.
Rows 4 and 5: As rows 2 and 3 but using yarn C in place of yarn B.
Row 6 (RS): Using yarn A K1, *P1, K1, rep from * to end.
Row 7: P1, *K1, P1, rep from * to end.
Cast off in rib (on **RS**).
See information page for finishing instructions, setting in sleeves using the set-in method.

BODY CHART

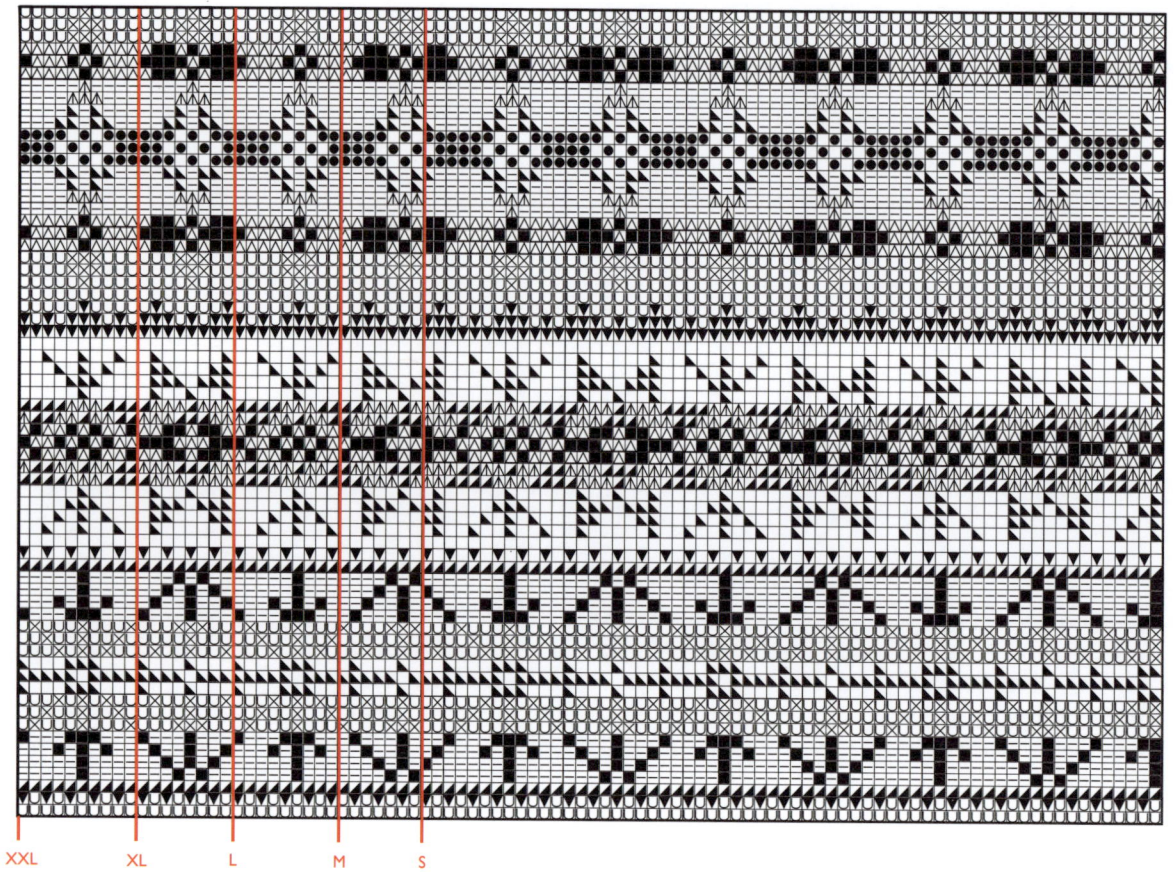

XXL   XL   L   M   S

SLEEVE CHART

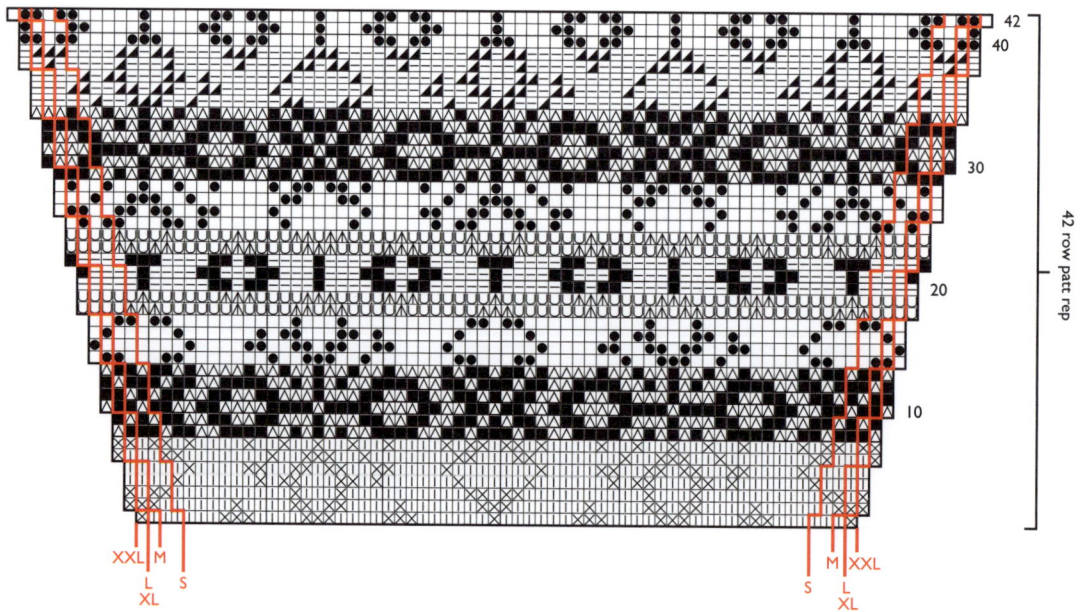

42
40

30

42 row patt rep

20

10

XXL M   S   S M XXL
L   L
XL   XL

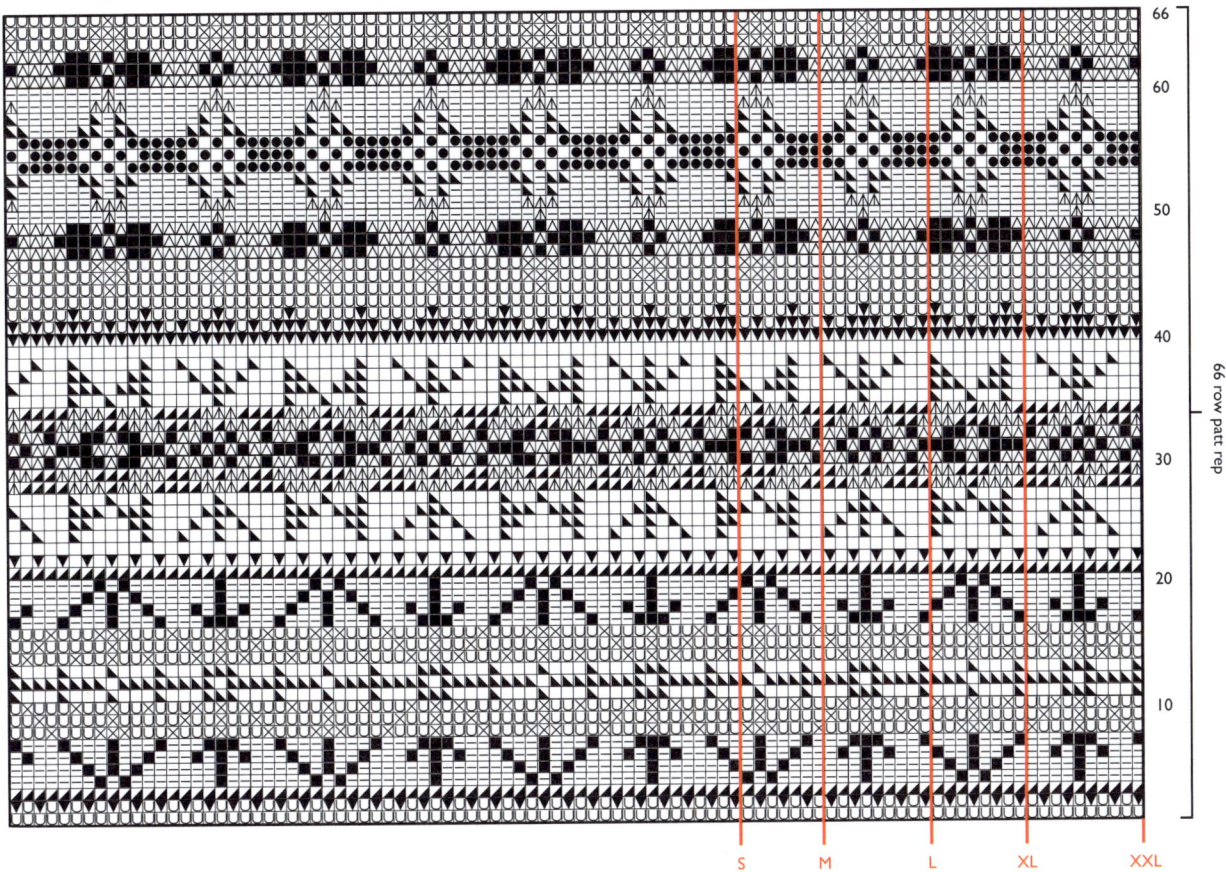

66 row patt rep

S M L XL XXL

KEY

∪ A. Silver Birch   ◢ C. Rose   ■ E. Wood   □ G. Quince   ∧ I. Foxglove   ● K. Chestnut

▼ B. Mallard   D. Eau de Nil   ✕ F. Dark Apple ◣ II. Russet   △ J. Pale Oak   ı L. Lime Flower

LUPIN SOCKS ● ●

Size
To fit average size woman's foot

Marie Wallin British Breeds

A	Eau de Nil	1	x 25gm
B	Russet	1	x 25gm
C	Lime Flower	1	x 25gm
D	Wood	1	x 25gm
E	Foxglove	1	x 25gm
F	Raw	2	x 25gm
G	Dark Apple	1	x 25gm
H	Silver Birch	1	x 25gm
I	Mulberry	1	x 25gm
J	Blossom	1	x 25gm
K	Quince	1	x 25gm
L	Chestnut	1	x 25gm
M	Pale Oak	1	x 25gm

Needles
Set of 5 double-pointed 2¾mm (no 12) (US 2) needles **or** 2¾mm (no 12) (US 2) circular needle – 25 cm (10 in) fixed length.
Set of 5 double-pointed 3¼mm (no 10) (US 3) needles **or** 3¼mm (no 10) (US 3) circular needle – 25 cm (10 in) fixed length.

Tension
28 sts and 29 rounds to 10 cm measured over patterned st st

using 3¼mm (US 3) needles.
LEFT SOCK
Using set of double-pointed 2¾mm (US 2) needles and yarn F cast on 62 sts.
Distribute sts evenly over 4 of the 5 needles and, using 5th needle and taking care not to twist cast-on edge, work in rounds as folls:
Round 1 (RS): *P1, K1, rep from * to end.
Place marker between first and last sts of round just knitted to denote beg and end of rounds – this marker "sits" along inside of leg.
Join in yarn D and stranding yarn not in use across **WS** of work (this is front of work on WS rows, and back of work on RS rows), now work in striped 2 colour rib as folls:

Round 2: *Using yarn F P1, using yarn D K1, rep from * to end.
Rep last round 8 times more.
Break off yarn D.
Rounds 11 and 12: As round 1.
Change to set of double-pointed 3¼mm (US 3) needles.**
Beg and ending rounds as indicated, using the **fairisle technique** as described on the information page and reading every chart round from right to left, cont in patt from chart, which is worked entirely in st st (K every round), as folls:
Work 4 rounds.
Inc 1 st at each end of next round. 64 sts.

Work 23 rounds.
Dec 1 st at each end of next and foll 12th round. 60 sts.
Work 11 rounds, ending after chart round 51.

Work heel
Slip first 30 sts of last round onto a holder – these will be used later for top of foot.
Join in yarn F.
Now working backwards and forwards in rows, not rounds, using yarn F **only** work heel on rem 30 sts as folls:
***Row 1 (RS):** K29, wrap next st (by slipping next st from left needle onto right needle, taking yarn to opposite side of work between needles and then slipping same st back onto left needle - when working back across wrapped sts work the wrapped st and the wrapping loop tog as one st) and turn.
Row 2: P28, wrap next st and turn.
Row 3: K27, wrap next st and turn.
Row 4: P26, wrap next st and turn.
Row 5: K25, wrap next st and turn.
Row 6: P24, wrap next st and turn.
Row 7: K23, wrap next st and turn.
Row 8: P22, wrap next st and turn.
Row 9: K21, wrap next st and turn.
Row 10: P20, wrap next st and turn.
Row 11: K19, wrap next st and turn.
Row 12: P18, wrap next st and turn.
Row 13: K17, wrap next st and turn.
Row 14: P16, wrap next st and turn.
Row 15: K15, wrap next st and turn.
Row 16: P14, wrap next st and turn.
Row 17: As row 15.
Row 18: As row 14.
Row 19: As row 13.
Row 20: As row 12.
Row 21: As row 11.
Row 22: As row 10.
Row 23: As row 9.
Row 24: As row 8.
Row 25: As row 7.
Row 26: As row 6.
Row 27: As row 5.
Row 28: As row 4.
Row 29: As row 3.
Row 30: As row 2.
Row 31: As row 1.
Row 32: P30.
Break off yarn F – heel is now completed.
Distribute all 60 sts evenly over 4 of the 5 needles again as before and, using 5th needle and taking care to beg these new rounds in same place as previous rounds, now start to work in rounds again from chart as folls:
(**Note**: To avoid a hole forming at heel "corner", you may like to pick up and knit 1 st from row-end edge of heel. Immediately slip this picked-up st onto left needle and then K this st tog with next st.)
Work chart rounds 52 to 96.

Shape toe
Break off contrasts and cont using yarn F **only**.
Rounds 1 and 2 (RS): Knit.
Round 3: (K1, sl 1, K1, psso, K24, K2tog, K1) twice. 56 sts.
Round 4: Knit.
Round 5: (K1, sl 1, K1, psso, K22, K2tog, K1) twice. 52 sts.
Round 6: Knit.
Round 7: (K1, sl 1, K1, psso, K20, K2tog, K1) twice. 48 sts.
Round 8: (K1, sl 1, K1, psso, K18, K2tog, K1) twice. 44 sts.
Round 9: (K1, sl 1, K1, psso, K16, K2tog, K1) twice. 40 sts.
Round 10: (K1, sl 1, K1, psso, K14, K2tog, K1) twice. 36 sts.
Round 11: (K1, sl 1, K1, psso, K12, K2tog, K1) twice. 32 sts.
Round 12: (K1, sl 1, K1, psso, K10, K2tog, K1) twice. 28 sts.
Break yarn. Slip first 14 sts and last 14 sts of last round onto a needle each and then graft toe closed using Kitchener st or grafting st.

RIGHT SOCK
Work as given for left sock to **.
Beg and ending rounds as indicated and reading every chart row from **left to right** (to reverse design for right sock), cont in patt from chart, which is worked entirely in st st (K every round), and work as given for left sock to start of heel shaping.
Work heel
Slip **last** 30 sts of last round onto a holder – these will be used later for top of foot.
Join in yarn F.
Now working backwards and forwards in rows, not rounds, using yarn F **only** work heel on **first** 30 sts as folls:
Complete right sock as given for left sock from *** to end.

MAKING UP
Press as described on the information page.
See information page for finishing instructions.

KEY

- **•** A. Eau de Nil
- **▲** B. Russet
- **╱** C Lime Flower
- **■** D. Wood
- **+** E. Foxglove
- **▢** F. Raw
- **◣** G. Dark Apple
- **−** H. Silver Birch
- **●** I. Mulberry
- **○** J. Blossom
- **|** K. Quince
- **▼** L. Chestnut
- **✕** M. Pale Oak

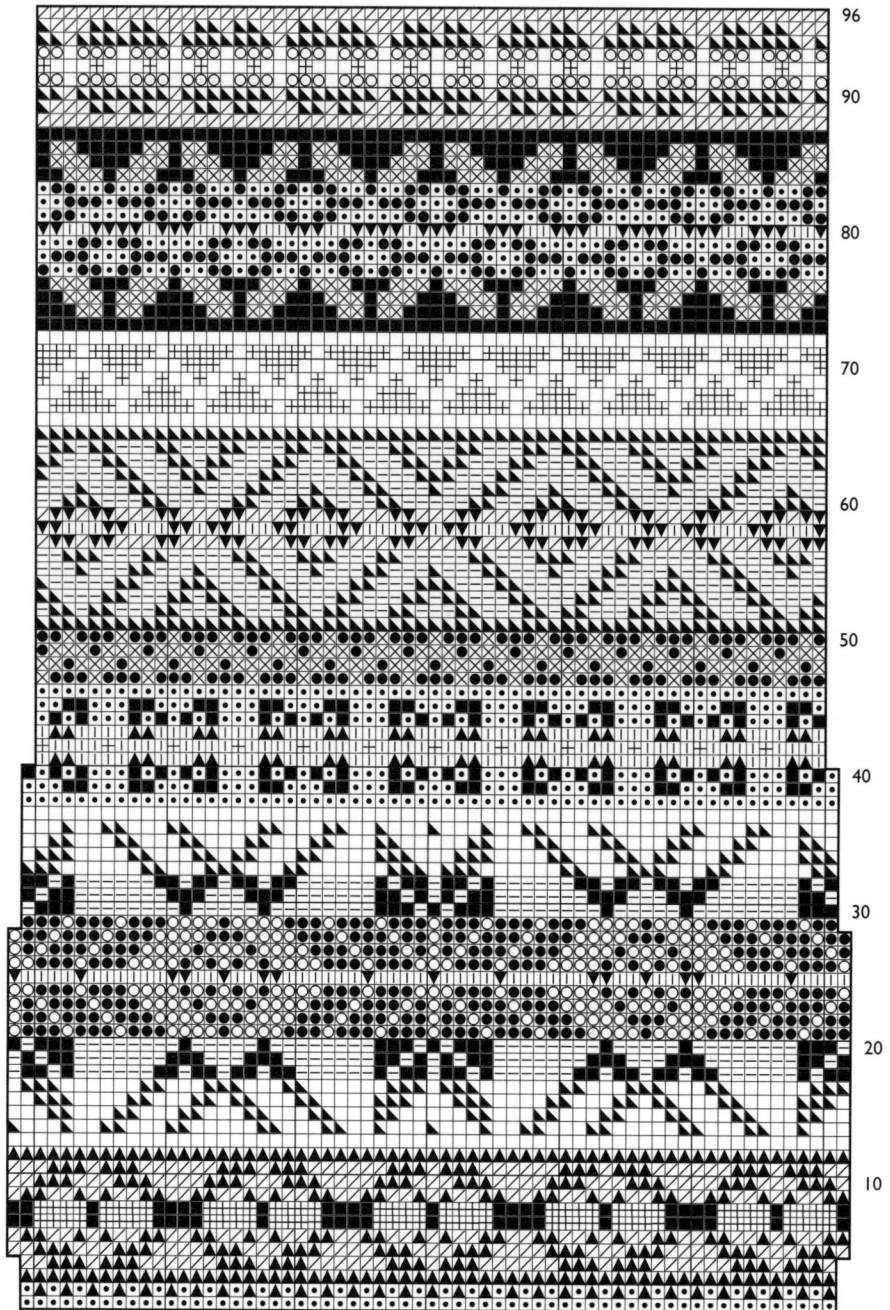

96
90
80
70
60
50
40
30
20
10

ORLA

● ● ●

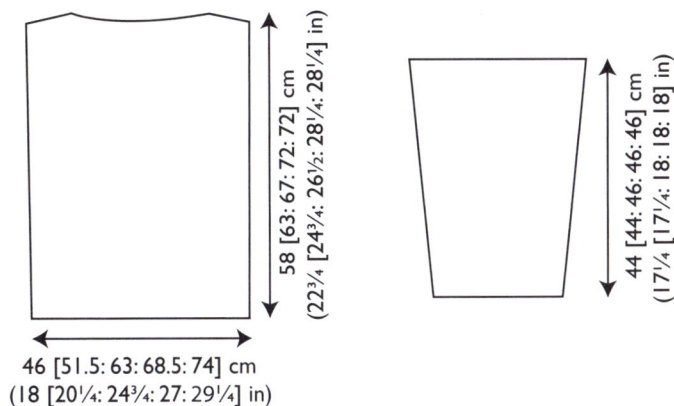

58 [63: 67: 72: 72] cm
(22¾ [24¾: 26½: 28¼: 28¼] in)

46 [51.5: 63: 68.5: 74] cm
(18 [20¼: 24¾: 27: 29¼] in)

44 [44: 46: 46: 46] cm
(17¼ [17¼: 18: 18: 18] in)

	S	M	L	XL	XXL	
To fit bust						
	81-86	91-97	102-117	122-127	132-137	cm
	32-34	36-38	40-46	48-50	52-54	

Marie Wallin British Breeds

A Quince	2	3	3	3	4	x 25gm
B Mallard	4	4	5	6	6	x 25gm
C Lime Flower	2	3	3	4	4	x 25gm
D Russet	3	3	4	4	4	x 25gm
E Pale Oak	2	2	2	3	3	x 25gm
F Chestnut	4	4	5	6	6	x 25gm
G Foxglove	2	2	3	3	3	x 25gm
H Dark Apple	4	4	5	6	6	x 25gm
I Mulberry	3	4	4	5	5	x 25gm
J Silver Birch	2	2	2	3	3	x 25gm
K Blossom	2	2	2	3	3	x 25gm

CROCHET HOOK and NEEDLES

2.50mm (no 12) (US B1/C2) crochet hook
1 pair 2¾mm (no 12) (US 2) needles
2¾mm (no 12) (US 2) circular needle
Set of 4 double-pointed 2¾mm (no 12) (US 2) needles

TENSION

25 sts and 21 rows to 10 cm measured over patt using 2.50mm (US B1/C2) crochet hook. Basic motif is 8 cm square using

2.50mm (US B1/C2) crochet hook.

CROCHET ABBREVIATIONS

ch = chain; **dc** = double crochet; **dc2tog** = (insert hook as indicated, yoh and draw loop through) twice, yoh and draw through all 3 loops; **htr** = half treble; **sp(s)** = space(s); **ss** = slip stitch; **tr** = treble; **tr2tog** = (yoh and insert hook as indicated, yoh and draw loop through, yoh and draw through 2 loops) twice, yoh and draw through all 3 loops; **tr3tog** = (yoh and insert hook as indicated, yoh and draw loop through, yoh and draw through 2 loops) 3 times, yoh and draw through all 4 loops; **yoh** = yarn over hook.

BASIC MOTIF
Using 2.50mm (US B1/C2) crochet hook and first colour, make 4 ch and join with a ss to form a ring.
Joining in and breaking off colours as required, cont as folls:
Round 1 (RS): Using first colour, 5 ch (counts as 1 tr and 2 ch), (1 tr into ring, 2 ch) 7 times, ss to 3rd of 5 ch at beg of round. 8 ch sps.
Round 2: Using second colour, ss into first ch sp, 3 ch (does NOT count as st), (tr2tog, 3 ch and tr3tog) into ch sp at base of 3 ch, *5 ch, 1 dc into next ch sp, 5 ch**, (tr3tog, 3 ch and tr3tog) into next ch sp, rep from * to end, ending last rep at **, ss to top of tr2tog at beg of round.
Round 3: Using third colour, ss into first ch sp, 3 ch (does NOT count as st), (tr2tog, 5 ch and tr3tog) into ch sp at base of 3 ch,

*(5 ch, 1 dc into next ch sp) twice, 5 ch**, (tr3tog, 5 ch and tr3tog) into next ch sp, rep from * to end, ending last rep at **, ss to top of tr2tog at beg of round. 16 ch sps.

Round 4: Using fourth colour, ss into first ch sp, 3 ch (does NOT count as st), (tr2tog, 7 ch and tr3tog) into ch sp at base of 3 ch, *5 ch, 1 dc into next ch sp, 5 ch, (tr3tog, 5 ch and tr3tog) into next ch sp, 5 ch, 1 dc into next ch sp, 5 ch**, (tr3tog, 7 ch and tr3tog) into next ch sp, rep from * to end, ending last rep at **, ss to top of tr2tog at beg of round.

Fasten off.

Basic motif is a square. In each corner there is a 7-ch sp and there are five 5-ch sps along each side between corner ch sps – 24 ch sps in total.

Join motifs whilst working round 4 by replacing each (5 ch) with (2 ch, 1 ss into corresponding ch sp of adjacent motif, 2 ch), and each (7 ch) with (3 ch, 1 ss into corresponding ch sp of adjacent motif, 3 ch).

Motifs are made in 2 different colourways: **For first colourway** use yarn A as first colour, yarn B as second colour, yarn C as third colour and yarn D as fourth colour. **For second colourway** use yarn E as first colour, yarn F as second colour, yarn G as third colour and yarn H as fourth colour.

BODY MOTIF BORDER
Make and join 12 [14: 16: 18: 20] basic motifs to form a loop – make 6 [7: 8: 9: 10] in each colourway and join motifs so that colourways alternate all around loop.

Lower trim and ribbing
With RS facing, 2.50mm (US B1/C2) crochet hook and yarn I, attach yarn to one corner ch sp of lower edge of joined motif loop, 1 ch (does NOT count as st), 2 dc into ch sp where yarn was attached, *1 dc into next tr3tog, 2 dc into each of next 2 ch sps, 1 dc into next tr3tog, 2 dc into next ch sp**, (1 dc into next tr3tog, 2 dc into each of next 2 ch sps) twice, rep from * to end, ending last rep at **, 1 dc into next tr3tog, 2 dc into each of next 2 ch sps, 1 dc into next tr3tog, 2 dc into next ch sp, ss to first dc. 216 [252: 288: 324: 360] sts, with 18 dc across top of each motif.

Round 1 (RS): 5 ch (counts as 1 tr and 2 ch), miss st at base of 5 ch and next 2 dc, *1 tr into next dc, 2 ch, miss 2 dc, rep from * to end, ss to 3rd of 5 ch at beg of round.

Round 2: 1 ch (does NOT count as st), 1 dc into same place as ss at end of previous round, *2 dc into next ch sp, 1 dc into next tr, rep from * to end, replacing dc at end of last rep with ss to first dc.***

Round 3: 1 ch (does NOT count as st), 1 dc into each dc to end, ss to first dc.

Fasten off.

With RS facing, using yarn J and 2¾mm (US 2) circular needle, pick up and knit 1 st for each dc around top of round 3. 216 [252: 288: 324: 360] sts.

****Round 1 (RS):** *K2, P2, rep from * to end.
This round forms rib.
Keeping rib correct and joining and breaking off colours as required, cont in striped rib as folls:
Rounds 2 and 3: Using yarn B.

Rounds 4 and 5: Using yarn K.
Rounds 6 and 7: Using yarn H.
Rounds 8 and 9: Using yarn F.
Rounds 10 and 11: Using yarn A.
Rounds 12 and 13: Using yarn B.
Rounds 14 and 15: Using yarn G.
Rounds 16 and 17: Using yarn I.
Rounds 18 and 19: Using yarn E.
Rounds 20 and 21: Using yarn D.
Rounds 22 and 23: Using yarn H.
Rounds 24 and 25: Using yarn C.
Rounds 26 and 27: Using yarn F.
Rounds 28 and 29: Using yarn J.
Using yarn J, cast off in rib.

Upper trim
Working along upper edge of joined motif loop, work as given for lower trim and ribbing to ***.
Fasten off.

BACK
Decide which colourway motif you want as the centre front motif (this can be either colourway) and fold body motif border flat, positioning chosen motif at centre of folded band - there will be 2½ [3: 3½: 4: 4½] motifs either side of this centre motif. Folds will become the base of side seams for upper back and front sections. Place markers at folds – this will be midway across top of a motif for sizes S, L and XXL and directly above motif joining point for sizes M and XL - there should be 108 [126: 144: 162: 180] sts between markers.

With RS facing, 2.50mm (US B1/C2) crochet hook and yarn I, attach yarn at right side seam marker and work across back upper edge to left side seam marker as folls: 1 ch (does NOT count as st), 1 dc into each of next 5 [20: 5: 8: 17] dc, 2 dc into next dc, (1 dc into each of next 15 [41: 10: 17: 35] dc, 2 dc into next dc) 6 [2: 12: 8: 4] times, 1 dc into each of next 6 [21: 6: 9: 18] dc, turn. 115 [129: 157: 171: 185] sts.

*****Joining in and breaking off colours as required, now work in patt as folls:

Row 1 (WS): Using yarn J, 2 ch (counts as 1 htr), 1 htr into st at base of 2 ch, *miss 1 dc, (1 htr, 1 ch and 1 htr) into next dc, rep from * to last 2 sts, miss 1 dc, 2 htr into last dc, turn.

Row 2: Using yarn B, 3 ch (does NOT count as st), 1 tr into st at base of 3 ch, *1 ch, miss 2 htr**, tr3tog into next ch sp, rep from * to end, ending last rep at **, tr2tog into top of 2 ch at beg of previous row, turn.

Row 3: Using yarn K, 2 ch (counts as 1 htr), miss st at base of 2 ch, *(1 htr, 1 ch and 1 htr) into next ch sp**, miss 1 tr3tog, rep from * to end, ending last rep at **, 1 htr into top of 3 ch at beg of previous row, turn.

Row 4: Using yarn H, 1 ch (does NOT count as st), 1 dc into htr at base of 1 ch, *miss 1 htr, 1 dc into next ch sp**, 1 dc into next htr, rep from * to end, ending last rep at **, miss 1 htr, 1 dc into top of 2 ch at beg of previous row, turn.

Row 5: Using yarn H, 1 ch (does NOT count as st), 1 dc into each dc to end, turn.

Row 6: Using yarn F, 3 ch (counts as 1 htr and 1 ch), miss first 2 dc, *1 dc into next dc, 3 ch, miss 3 dc, 1 dc into next dc**, 3 ch, miss 2 dc, rep from * to end, ending last rep at **, 1 ch, miss 2 dc, 1 htr into last dc, turn.

Row 7: Using yarn F, 1 ch (does NOT count as st), 1 dc into htr at base of 1 ch, *1 ch, miss 1 dc, (1 tr, 1 ch, 1 tr, 1 ch, 1 tr, 1 ch and 1 tr) into next ch sp, 1 ch, miss 1 dc, 1 dc into next ch sp, rep from * to end, working dc at end of last rep into 2nd of 3 ch at beg of previous row, turn. 16 [18: 22: 24: 26] patt repeats.

Row 8: Using yarn A, 4 ch (counts as 1 tr and 1 ch), miss (dc at base of 4 ch, 1 ch and 1 tr), *1 dc into next ch sp, 3 ch, miss (1 tr, 1 ch and 1 tr), 1 dc into next ch sp**, 3 ch, miss (1 tr, 1 ch, 1 dc, 1 ch and 1 tr), rep from * to end, ending last rep at **, 1 ch, miss (1 tr and 1 ch), 1 tr into last dc, turn.

Row 9: Using yarn A, 3 ch (counts as 1 tr), miss tr at base of 3 ch, (1 tr, 1 ch and 1 tr) into first ch sp, *1 ch, miss 1 dc, 1 dc into next ch sp, 1 ch, miss 1 dc**, (1 tr, 1 ch, 1 tr, 1 ch, 1 tr, 1 ch and 1 tr) into next ch sp, rep from * to end, ending last rep at **, (1 tr, 1 ch and 1 tr) into last ch sp, 1 tr into 3rd of 4 ch at beg of previous row, turn.

Row 10: Using yarn B, 3 ch (counts as 1 htr and 1 ch), miss first 2 tr, *1 dc into next ch sp, 3 ch, miss (1 tr, 1 ch, 1 dc, 1 ch and 1 tr), 1 dc into next ch sp**, 3 ch, miss (1 tr, 1 ch and 1 tr), rep from * to end, ending last rep at **, 1 ch, miss 1 tr, 1 htr into top of 3 ch at beg of previous row, turn.

Row 11: Using yarn B, 1 ch (does NOT count as st), 1 dc into htr at base of 1 ch, 2 dc into first ch sp, *miss 1 dc, 4 dc into next ch sp, miss 1 dc**, 3 dc into next ch sp, rep from * to end, ending last rep at **, 2 dc into last ch sp, 1 dc into 2nd of 3 ch at beg of previous row, turn.
These 11 rows form patt.
(**Note**: The number of sts varies whilst working patt. Count sts after rows 4, 5 and 11 **only**. All st counts given relate to original number of sts and do **NOT** take into account sts lost or made whilst working patt.)
Keeping patt correct as now set, cont in stripes as folls:
Row 12 (RS): Using yarn G.
Row 13: Using yarn I.
Row 14: Using yarn E.
Rows 15 and 16: Using yarn D.
Rows 17 and 18: Using yarn H.
Rows 19 and 20: Using yarn C.
Rows 21 and 22: Using yarn F.
Last 22 rows form stripe sequence.
Keeping the 11 row patt repeat correct and the 22 row stripe sequence correct throughout as now set, cont as folls:****
Work in patt for a further 44 [55: 66: 77: 77] rows, ending after patt row 11. 115 [129: 157: 171: 185] sts.
Keeping stripe sequence correct, cont in patt as folls:
Shape neck
Row 1: 2 ch (counts as 1 htr), 1 htr into st at base of 2 ch, *miss 1 dc, (1 htr, 1 ch and 1 htr) into next dc, rep from * 16 [19: 26: 30: 33] times more, miss 2 dc, 1 tr into next dc, turn.
Work each side of neck separately as folls:
Row 2: 3 ch (counts as 1 tr), miss (1 tr, 1 htr, 1 ch sp and 2 htr),

(tr3tog into next ch sp, 1 ch, miss 2 htr) 16 [19: 26: 30: 33] times, tr2tog into top of 2 ch at beg of previous row, turn.
Row 3: 2 ch (counts as 1 htr), miss st at base of 2 ch, *(1 htr, 1 ch and 1 htr) into next ch sp, miss 1 tr3tog, rep from * 14 [17: 24: 28: 31] times more, miss last (ch sp and tr3tog), 1 tr into top of 3 ch at beg of previous row, turn.
Row 4: 1 ch (does NOT count as st), miss (1 tr and 1 htr), (1 dc into next ch sp, 1 dc into next htr, miss 1 htr) 14 [17: 24: 28: 31] times, 1 dc into next ch sp, 1 dc into top of 2 ch at beg of previous row, turn. 30 [36: 50: 58: 64] sts.
Row 5: 1 ch (does NOT count as st), 1 dc into each of next 28 [34: 48: 56: 62] dc, dc2tog over last 2 dc, turn. 29 [35: 49: 57: 63] sts.
Row 6: 1 ch (does NOT count as st), 1 dc into first st, 3 ch, miss 3 [2: 2: 3: 2] dc, 1 dc into next dc, (3 ch, miss 2 dc, 1 dc into next dc, 3 ch, miss 3 dc, 1 dc into next dc) 3 [4: 6: 7: 8] times, 2 ch, miss 2 dc, 1 htr into last dc, turn. 8 [10: 14: 16: 18] ch sps.
Row 7: 3 ch (counts as 1 tr), miss st at base of 3 ch, 2 tr into first ch sp, (miss 1 dc, 4 tr into next ch sp, miss 1 dc, 3 tr into next ch sp) 3 [4: 6: 7: 8] times, miss 1 dc, 1 tr into next ch sp, tr2tog working first 'leg' into same ch sp as previous tr and second 'leg' into last dc, turn. 26 [33: 47: 54: 61] sts.
Row 8: 1 ch (does NOT count as st), 1 dc into each st to end, working last dc into top of 3 ch at beg of previous row.
Fasten off.
Return to last complete row worked, miss centre 39 [41: 41: 39: 41] dc, attach appropriate yarn to next dc and cont as folls:
Row 1: 3 ch (counts as 1 tr), miss (dc at base of 3 ch and next 2 dc), *(1 htr, 1 ch and 1 htr) into next dc, miss 1 dc, rep from * 16 [19: 26: 30: 33] times more, 2 htr into last dc, turn.
Row 2: 3 ch (does NOT count as st), 1 tr into st at base of 3 ch, (1 ch, miss 2 htr, tr3tog into next ch sp) 16 [19: 26: 30: 33] times, miss (2 htr, 1 ch sp and 1 htr), 1 tr into top of 3 ch at beg of previous row, turn.
Row 3: 3 ch (counts as 1 tr), miss (st at base of 3 ch, 1 tr3tog, 1 ch sp and 1 tr3tog), *(1 htr, 1 ch and 1 htr) into next ch sp, miss 1 tr3tog, rep from * 13 [16: 23: 27: 30] times more, (1 htr, 1 ch and 1 htr) into last ch sp, 1 htr into top of 3 ch at beg of previous row, turn.
Row 4: 1 ch (does NOT count as st), 1 dc into htr at base of 1 ch, (miss 1 htr, 1 dc into next ch sp, 1 dc into next htr) 14 [17: 24: 28: 31] times, miss 1 htr, dc2tog working first 'leg' into last ch sp and second 'leg' into top of 3 ch at beg of previous row, turn.
30 [36: 50: 58: 64] sts.
Row 5: 1 ch (does NOT count as st), miss st at base of 1 ch, 1 dc into each of next 29 [35: 49: 57: 63] dc, turn. 29 [35: 49: 57: 63] sts.
Row 6: 4 ch (counts as 1 htr and 2 ch), miss first 3 dc, 1 dc into next dc, (3 ch, miss 3 dc, 1 dc into next dc, 3 ch, miss 2 dc, 1 dc into next dc) 3 [4: 6: 7: 8] times, 3 ch, miss 3 [2: 2: 3: 2] dc, 1 dc into last dc, turn. 8 [10: 14: 16: 18] ch sps.
Row 7: 3 ch (does NOT count as st), miss dc at base of 3 ch, 2 tr into first ch sp, (miss 1 dc, 3 tr into next ch sp, miss 1 dc, 4 tr into next ch sp) 3 [4: 6: 7: 8] times, miss 1 dc, 2 tr into last ch sp, 1 tr into 2nd of 4 ch at beg of previous row, turn.
26 [33: 47: 54: 61] sts.

Row 8: 1 ch (does NOT count as st), 1 dc into each st to end, omitting 3 ch at beg of previous row.
Fasten off.

FRONT
With RS facing, 2.50mm (US B1/C2) crochet hook and yarn I, attach yarn at left side seam marker and work across front upper edge to right side seam marker as folls: 1 ch (does NOT count as st), 1 dc into each of next 5 [20: 5: 8: 17] dc, 2 dc into next dc, (1 dc into each of next 15 [41: 10: 17: 35] dc, 2 dc into next dc) 6 [2: 12: 8: 4] times, 1 dc into each of next 6 [21: 6: 9: 18] dc, turn. 115 [129: 157: 171: 185] sts.
Complete as given for back from *****.

SLEEVE MOTIF BORDERS
Make and join 3 [3: 3: 4: 4] basic motifs to form a loop – make 1 [1: 1: 2: 2] in first colourway and 2 in second colourway, and join motifs so that for sizes S, M and L the first colourway is at "centre", and for sizes XL and XXL the colourways alternate around loop.

Lower trim and ribbing
Working around lower edge of joined motifs, work as given for lower trim of body motif border to ***, **noting** that there will be 54 [54: 54: 72: 72] sts, with 18 dc across top of each motif.
Round 3: 1 ch (does NOT count as st), 1 dc into each dc to end, ss to first dc.
Fasten off.
With RS facing, using yarn J and set of 4 double-pointed 2¾mm (US 2) needles, pick up and knit 1 st for each dc around top of round 3, **omitting 2 [2: 2: 4: 4] dc evenly around.**
52 [52: 52: 68: 68] sts.
Complete as given for lower trim and ribbing of body from ****.
Upper trim
Work as given for upper trim of body motif border to ***, **noting** that there will be 54 [54: 54: 72: 72] sts, with 18 dc across top of each motif.
Fasten off.

SLEEVES
Sizes S, M and L only
Place a marker between 2 dc on upper trim directly above the joining point between the two motifs in second colourway – this denotes the sleeve seam position.
Sizes XL and XXL only
Place a marker between 2 dc on upper trim directly above the joining point between a motif in first colourway and a motif in second colourway – this denotes the sleeve seam position.
All sizes
With RS facing, 2.50mm (US B1/C2) crochet hook and yarn I, attach yarn in dc to the left of marker and work across 54 [54: 54: 72: 72] sts of upper edge as folls: 1 ch (does NOT count as st), 1 dc into each of next 5 [5: 5: 35: 35] dc, 2 dc into next dc, (1 dc into each of next 10 dc, 2 dc into next dc) 4 [4: 4: 0: 0] times, 1 dc into each of last 4 [4: 4: 36: 36] dc, turn. 59 [59: 59: 73: 73] sts.

Joining in and breaking off colours as required, now work in patt and shape sides as folls:
Row 1 (WS): Using yarn J, 2 ch (counts as 1 htr), 1 htr into st at base of 2 ch, *miss 1 dc, (1 htr, 1 ch and 1 htr) into next dc, rep from * to last 2 sts, miss 1 dc, 2 htr into last dc, turn.
Row 2: Using yarn B, 3 ch (does NOT count as st), 1 tr into st at base of 3 ch, *1 ch, miss 2 htr**, tr3tog into next ch sp, rep from * to end, ending last rep at **, tr2tog into top of 2 ch at beg of previous row, turn.
Row 3: Using yarn K, 2 ch (counts as 1 htr), miss st at base of 2 ch, *(1 htr, 1 ch and 1 htr) into next ch sp**, miss 1 tr3tog, rep from * to end, ending last rep at **, 1 htr into top of 3 ch at beg of previous row, turn.
Row 4: Using yarn H, 1 ch (does NOT count as st), 1 dc into htr at base of 1 ch, *miss 1 htr, 1 dc into next ch sp**, 1 dc into next htr, rep from * to end, ending last rep at **, miss 1 htr, 1 dc into top of 2 ch at beg of previous row, turn. 59 [59: 59: 73: 73] sts.
Row 5: Using yarn H, 1 ch (does NOT count as st), 1 dc into each dc to end, **working 2 dc into 7 dc evenly across row** – 7 sts increased, turn. 66 [66: 66: 80: 80] sts.
Row 6: Using yarn F, 3 ch (counts as 1 htr and 1 ch), miss first 2 dc, *1 dc into next dc, 3 ch, miss 3 dc, 1 dc into next dc**, 3 ch, miss 2 dc, rep from * to end, ending last rep at **, 1 ch, miss 2 dc, 1 htr into last dc, turn.
Row 7: Using yarn F, 1 ch (does NOT count as st), 1 dc into htr at base of 1 ch, *1 ch, miss 1 dc, (1 tr, 1 ch, 1 tr, 1 ch, 1 tr, 1 ch and 1 tr) into next ch sp, 1 ch, miss 1 dc, 1 dc into next ch sp, rep from * to end, working dc at end of last rep into 2nd of 3 ch at beg of previous row, turn. 9 [9: 9: 11: 11] patt repeats.
Row 8: Using yarn A, 4 ch (counts as 1 tr and 1 ch), miss (dc at base of 4 ch, 1 ch and 1 tr), *1 dc into next ch sp, 3 ch, miss (1 tr, 1 ch and 1 tr), 1 dc into next ch sp**, 3 ch, miss (1 tr, 1 ch, 1 dc, 1 ch and 1 tr), rep from * to end, ending last rep at **, 1 ch, miss (1 tr and 1 ch), 1 tr into last dc, turn.
Row 9: Using yarn A, 3 ch (counts as 1 tr), miss tr at base of 3 ch, (1 tr, 1 ch and 1 tr) into first ch sp, *1 ch, miss 1 dc, 1 dc into next ch sp, 1 ch, miss 1 dc**, (1 tr, 1 ch, 1 tr, 1 ch, 1 tr, 1 ch and 1 tr) into next ch sp, rep from * to end, ending last rep at **, (1 tr, 1 ch and 1 tr) into last ch sp, 1 tr into 3rd of 4 ch at beg of previous row, turn.
Row 10: Using yarn B, 3 ch (counts as 1 htr and 1 ch), miss first 2 tr, *1 dc into next ch sp, 3 ch, miss (1 tr, 1 ch, 1 dc, 1 ch and 1 tr), 1 dc into next ch sp**, 3 ch, miss (1 tr, 1 ch and 1 tr), rep from * to end, ending last rep at **, 1 ch, miss 1 tr, 1 htr into top of 3 ch at beg of previous row, turn.
Row 11: Using yarn B, 1 ch (does NOT count as st), 1 dc into htr at base of 1 ch, 2 dc into first ch sp, *miss 1 dc, 4 dc into next ch sp, miss 1 dc**, 3 dc into next ch sp, rep from * to end, ending last rep at **, 2 dc into last ch sp, 1 dc into 2nd of 3 ch at beg of previous row, turn.
Row 12: As row 1 using yarn G instead of yarn J.
Row 13: As row 2 using yarn I instead of yarn B.
Row 14: As row 3 using yarn E instead of yarn K.
Row 15: As row 4 using yarn D instead of yarn H.
Row 16: Using yarn D, 1 ch (does NOT count as st), 1 dc into

each dc to end, **working 2 dc into 7 dc evenly across row** –
6 sts increased, turn. 73 [73: 73: 87: 87] sts.
Row 17: As row 6 using yarn H instead of yarn F.
Row 18: As row 7 using yarn H instead of yarn F. 10 [10: 10: 12: 12] patt repeats.
Rows 19 and 20: As rows 8 and 9 using yarn C instead of yarn A.
Rows 21 and 22: As rows 10 and 11 using yarn F instead of yarn B.
These 22 rows form patt and stripe sequence with 14 sts increased in each 22 row repeat.
Rep last 22 rows once more, ending with **WS** facing for next row. 87 [87: 87: 101: 101] sts.
Size S only
Now work rows 1 to 11 in patt and stripe sequence as given for back, ending with RS facing for next row. 87 sts.
Size M only
Now work rows 1 to 11 of sleeve patt and stripe sequence once more, ending with RS facing for next row. 94 sts.
Sizes L, XL and XXL only
Now work rows 1 to 16 of sleeve patt and stripe sequence once more, ending with **WS** facing for next row. - [-: 101: 115: 115] sts.
All sizes
Fasten off.

MAKING UP
Press as described on the information page.
Join right shoulder seam using back stitch, or mattress stitch if preferred.
Neckband
With RS facing, using 2¾mm (US 2) needles and yarn J, pick up and knit 10 sts down left side of front neck, 39 sts across front, 10 sts up right side of front neck, and 10 sts down right side of back neck, 39 sts across back, then 10 sts up left side of back neck. 118 sts.
Row 1 (WS): P2, *K2, P2, rep from * to end.
Break off yarn J and join in yarn B.
Row 2: Using yarn B, K2, *P2, K2, rep from * to end.
These 2 rows form rib.
Keeping rib correct and joining and breaking off colours as required, cont in striped rib as folls:
Row 3: Using yarn B.
Rows 4 and 5: Using yarn H.
Row 6: Using yarn F.
Using yarn F, cast off in rib (on **WS**).
Join left shoulder and neckband seam. Mark points along side seam edges 18 [19.5: 21: 24: 24] cm either side of shoulder seams and sew top edge of sleeves to back and front between these points. Join side and sleeve seams from top of motif borders.

BEECH

● ● ●

56 [60: 62] cm
(22 [23½: 24½] in)

64 [76: 83] cm
(25¼ [30: 32¾] in)

32 [33: 33] cm
(12½ [13: 13:] in)

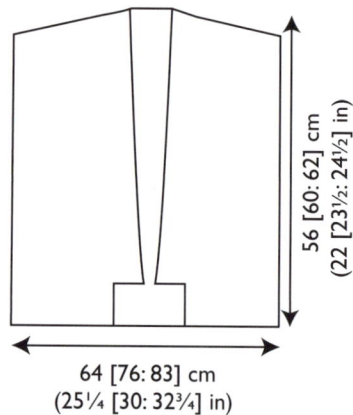

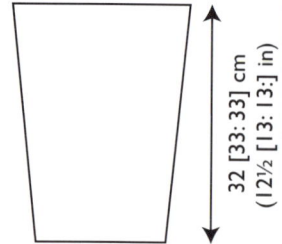

To fit bust	S-M	L-XL	XXL	
	81-97	102-117	122-127	cm
	32-38	40-46	48-50	in

Marie Wallin British Breeds

	22	28	31	x 25gm

(photographed in Rose)

Needles

1 pair 2¾mm (no 12) (US 2) needles
1 pair 3¼mm (no 10) (US 3) needles
2¾mm (no 12) (US 2) circular needle
3¼mm (no 10) (US 3) circular needle
Cable needle

Tension

42 sts and 43 rows to 10 cm measured over hem border patt,
40 sts and 41 rows to 10 cm measured over main patt, 39 sts and
39 rows to 10 cm measured over front band patt, all using 3¼mm
(US 3) needles.

Special abbreviations

C3B = slip next st onto cable needle and leave at back of work,
K2, then K1 from cable needle; **C3F** = slip next 2 sts onto cable
needle and leave at front of work, K1, then K2 from cable needle;
C4B = slip next 2 sts onto cable needle and leave at back of
work, K2, then K2 from cable needle; **C4F** = slip next 2 sts onto

cable needle and leave at front of work, K2, then K2 from cable
needle; **C6B** = slip next 3 sts onto cable needle and leave at back
of work, K3, then K3 from cable needle; **C6F** = slip next 3 sts onto
cable needle and leave at front of work, K3, then K3 from cable
needle; **C8B** = slip next 4 sts onto cable needle and leave at back
of work, K4, then K4 from cable needle; **C8F** = slip the next 4 sts
onto cable needle and leave at front of work, K4, then K4 from
the cable needle; **Cr3L** = slip next 2 sts onto cable needle and
leave at front of work, P1, then K2 from cable needle; **Cr3R** = slip
next st onto cable needle and leave at back of work, K2, then P1
from cable needle; **Cr4L** = slip next 2 sts onto cable needle and
leave at front of work, P2, then K2 from cable needle; **Cr4R** = slip
next 2 sts onto cable needle and leave at back of work, K2, then
P2 from cable needle; **Cr5L** = slip next 3 sts onto cable needle
and leave at front of work, P2, then K3 from cable needle; **Cr5R**
= slip next 2 sts onto cable needle and leave at back of work, K3,
then P2 from cable needle; **Tw2L** = K into back of second st on
left needle, K tog tbl first 2 sts on left needle and slip both sts off
left needle together; **Tw2R** = K2tog leaving sts on left needle, K
first st again and slip both sts off left needle together.

PATTERN NOTE
**Right rows are worked on 'even numbered' chart rows and
wrong side rows on 'odd numbered' chart rows.**

BODY (knitted in one piece)

First hem border section

Using 3¼mm (US 3) needles cast on 84 sts.

Beg and ending rows as indicated, **noting that chart row 1 is a WS row**, repeating the 24 st patt repeat 3 times across each row and the 24 row patt repeat throughout, now work in patt from chart A as folls:

Cont in patt until this border section meas 60 [72: 79] cm, ending with RS facing for next row.

Break yarn and leave sts on a holder.

Second hem border section

Using 3¼mm (US 3) needles cast on 84 sts.

Beg and ending rows as indicated, **noting that chart row 1 is a WS row**, repeating the 24 st patt repeat 3 times across each row and the 24 row patt repeat throughout, now work in patt from chart B as folls:

Cont in patt until this border section meas 60 [72: 79] cm, ending with RS facing for next row.

Join hem border sections

Holding hem border sections with their RS together and using a third 3¼mm (US 3) needle, cast off both sets of 84 sts together (to form centre back seam).

The upper long edge of joined hem border sections will form lower edge for upper body sections. Along this edge, place markers 28 [34: 37.5] cm from cast-on edges – there should be 64 [76: 83] cm between markers. These markers denote base of side seams.

Upper back

With RS facing and using 3¼mm (US 3) needles, pick up and knit 256 [304: 332] sts evenly along marked row-end edge of joined hem border sections between side seam markers.

Beg and ending rows as indicated, **noting that chart row 1 is a WS row**, repeating each 59 st patt repeat 1 [2: 2] times across each row and the 40 row patt repeat throughout, now work in patt from chart C as folls:

Cont straight until upper back meas 30.5 [34.5: 36.5] cm **from pick-up row**, ending with RS facing for next row.

Shape shoulders

Keeping patt correct, cast off 12 [15: 16] sts at beg of next 10 [16: 6] rows, then 13 [16: 17] sts at beg of foll 8 [2: 12] rows. Cast off rem 32 sts.

Upper left front

With RS facing and using 3¼mm (US 3) needles, pick up and knit 112 [136: 150] sts evenly along marked row-end edge of joined hem border sections, picking up sts from left side seam marker (this is base of left side seam edge of upper back) to one cast-on edge.

Beg and ending rows as indicated, **noting that chart row 1 is a WS row**, repeating each 59 st patt repeat 1 [2: 2] times across each row and the 40 row patt repeat throughout, now work in patt from chart C as folls:

Cont straight until upper left front matches upper back to beg of shoulder shaping, ending with RS facing for next row.

Shape shoulder

Keeping patt correct, cast off 12 [15: 16] sts at beg of next and

foll 4 [7: 2] alt rows, then 13 [-: 17] sts at beg of foll 3 [-: 5] alt rows.

Work 1 row.

Cast off rem 13 [16: 17] sts.

Upper right front

With RS facing and using 3¼mm (US 3) needles, pick up and knit 112 [136: 150] sts evenly along rem section of marked row-end edge of joined hem border sections, picking up sts from rem cast-on edge to right side seam marker (this is base of right side seam edge of upper back).

Complete to match upper left front, reversing shapings.

SLEEVES

Using 2¾mm (US 2) needles cast on 79 [83: 87] sts.

Row 1 (RS): K1, *P1, K1, rep from * to end.

Row 2: P1, *K1, P1, rep from * to end.

These 2 rows form rib.

Work in rib for a further 5 rows, inc 1 st at end of last row and ending with **WS** facing for next row. 80 [84: 88] sts.

Change to 3¼mm (US 3) needles.

Beg and ending rows as indicated, **noting that chart row 1 is a WS row** and repeating the 40 row patt repeat throughout, now work in patt from chart C as folls:

Inc 1 st at each end of 4th and every foll 4th row until there are 136 [152: 160] sts, taking inc sts into patt

Cont straight until sleeve meas 32 [33: 33] cm, ending with RS facing for next row.

Cast off.

MAKING UP

Press as described on the information page.

Join both shoulder seams using back stitch, or mattress stitch if preferred.

Front band

Mark points along front opening edges 9.5 cm up from lower (row-end) edge of joined hem border sections.

With RS facing and using 3¼mm (US 3) circular needle, beg and ending at these marked points, pick up and knit 174 [192: 198] sts up right front opening edge, 32 sts across back neck, and 174 [192: 198] sts down left front opening edge.
380 [416: 428] sts.

Row 1 (WS): K2, *P4, K2, rep from * to end.

Row 2: K1, P1, *C4B, P2, rep from * to last 6 sts, C4B, P1, K1.

Row 3: As row 1.

Row 4: K1, P1, *K4, P2, rep from * to last 6 sts, K4, P1, K1.

These 4 rows form front band patt.

Cont in front band patt for a further 27 rows, ending with RS facing for next row.

Cast off.

Hem and lower front edging

With RS facing and using 2¾mm (US 2) circular needle, beg and ending at end of cast-off edge of front band, pick up and knit 25 sts along left front row-end edge to front band pick-up row, pick up and knit 1 st from pick-up row and mark this st with a blue thread, pick up and knit 33 sts down rem free cast-on edge of hem border section, pick up and knit 1 st from corner and mark this st with a red thread, pick up and knit 397 [443: 487] sts along lower row-end edge of joined hem border section to cast-on edge at base of right front opening edge, pick up and knit 1 st from corner and mark this st with another red thread, pick up and knit 33 sts up rem free cast-on edge of this end of hem border section to front band pick-up row, pick up and knit 1 st from pick-up row and mark this st with another blue thread, and then pick up and knit 25 sts along right front row-end edge to front band cast-off edge. 517 [563: 607] sts.

Row 1 (WS): K1, *P1, K1, rep from * to end.
This row sets position of rib as given for cuff edges of sleeves.
Keeping rib correct, cont as folls:

Row 2: K1, *rib to within 1 st of blue marked st, slip next 2 sts as though to K2tog, K1, then pass 2 slipped sts over and reposition blue marker on this st*, (rib to red marked st, M1, K red marked st, M1) twice, rep from * to * once more, rib to last st, K1.

Row 3: K1, *rib to within 2 sts of blue marked st, work 2 tog, P blue marked st, work 2 tog tbl*, (rib to marked red st, M1, P marked st, M1) twice, rep from * to * once more, rib to last st, K1.
Rep last 2 rows once more.

Cast off in rib, still dec at blue marked sts and inc at red marked sts as before.

Mark points along side seam edges of upper front and back sections 18 [20: 21] cm below shoulder seams, then join side seams of these upper body sections from these marked points to pick-up rows at top of joined hem border sections. Join sleeve seams. Insert sleeves into armholes.

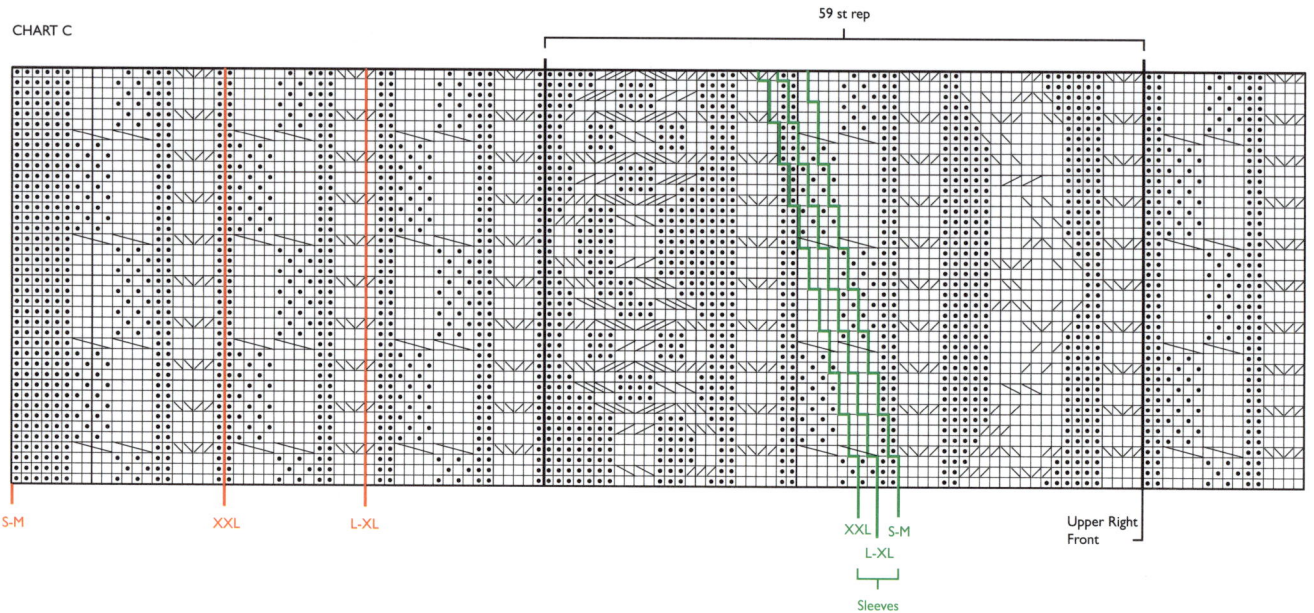

CHART C

59 st rep

S-M   XXL   L-XL

XXL S-M
L-XL
Sleeves

Upper Right Front

KEY

□	K on RS, P on WS	⧄	Cr4L
•	P on RS, K on WS	⧄	Cr4R
⧄	Tw2R	⧄	C4F
⧄	Tw2L	⧄	C4B
⧄	Cr3L	⧄	Cr5L
⧄	Cr3R	⧄	Cr5R
⧄	C3F	⧄	C6F
⧄	C3B	⧄	C6B
		⧄	C8B
		⧄	C8F

CHART A

24 st rep

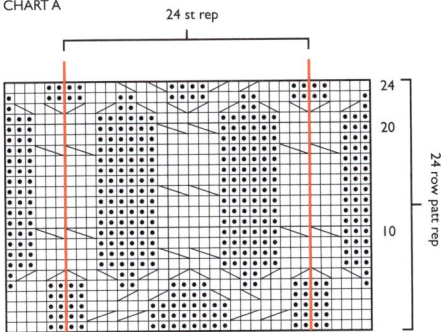

24
20

10

24 row patt rep

CHART B

24 st rep

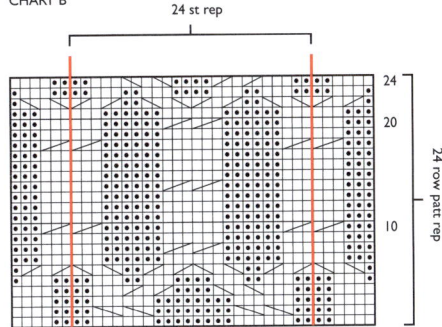

24
20

10

24 row patt rep

59 st rep

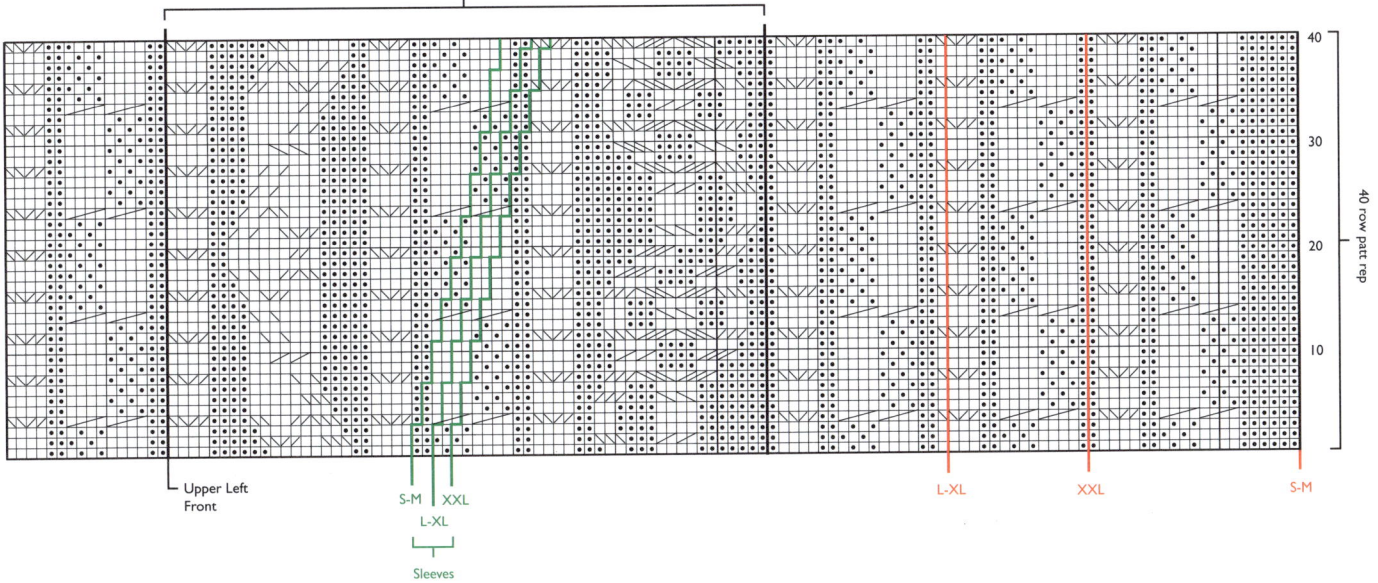

40

30

20

10

40 row patt rep

Upper Left
Front

S-M XXL
L-XL

Sleeves

L-XL   XXL   S-M